"The Apostle Paul models authentic Christ-centered leadership for the early church in his letters. His wisdom remains true and necessary for those leaders who desire to imitate and serve Christ. Benjamin Crisp's erudite and brilliant books on Paul's leadership principles in his first letter to the church in Corinth is essential reading for leaders focused on a Biblical recovery of authentic Christian leadership."

—CORNÉ J. BEKKER, Dean, Regent University School of Divinity

"It's exciting and encouraging to see, hear, and read young pastors engage the Biblical text for the sake of God's sheep under their charge. That is what Pastor Benjamin Crisp is doing in his ministry at Reflection Church. In this book we are reading the results of his hours of prayer and preparation as he goes about feeding the flock of God. Laced with practical insights and relevant illustrations, this book on 1 Corinthians is a must for every minister."

—A.D. BEACHAM JR., General Superintendent, International Pentecostal Holiness Church

"We live in an age of spiritual compromise. Many Christians today have 'deconstructed' their faith to make it fit with today's culture. And yet we have the example of the apostle Paul, who brought a radical, countercultural message to places like Corinth, Ephesus, and Rome. Paul didn't adjust his message to fit culture—instead, he warned his disciples not to conform to this world. I'm so grateful for young leaders like Benjamin Crisp. Instead of deconstructing his faith, he's challenging his generation to reclaim and reconstruct the New Testament faith we see in Paul's message to the Corinthians. This book is a powerful tool to train emerging ministry leaders."

—J. LEE GRADY, Director, The Mordecai Project

"There is often a disconnect between the current church and the Early church and some of the deeply profound mysteries, insights, and transformational truth is lost in the 2,000 years between those early Christian communities and ours here and now. Dr. Crisp does an exceptional job of bringing us back to that early Corinthian community both in its historical context and the apostolic letter written to them. The same truth that Paul is unveiling to them is shown to us here and now in this wonderful book. Every pastor, every Christian leader will greatly benefit from a thorough reading of this book."

—JOEL SOLOMON, Lead Pastor, New Life Church

*Strengthening the
Church and Its Leaders*

Strengthening the Church and Its Leaders

PAUL'S BLUEPRINT IN 1 CORINTHIANS

Benjamin Crisp

WIPF & STOCK · Eugene, Oregon

STRENGTHENING THE CHURCH AND ITS LEADERS
Paul's Blueprint in 1 Corinthians

Copyright © 2026 Benjamin Crisp. All rights reserved. Except for brief quotations in critical publications or reviews, no part of this book may be reproduced in any manner without prior written permission from the publisher. Write: Permissions, Wipf and Stock Publishers, 199 W. 8th Ave., Suite 3, Eugene, OR 97401.

Wipf & Stock
An Imprint of Wipf and Stock Publishers
199 W. 8th Ave., Suite 3
Eugene, OR 97401

www.wipfandstock.com

PAPERBACK ISBN: 979-8-3852-7213-6
HARDCOVER ISBN: 979-8-3852-7214-3
EBOOK ISBN: 979-8-3852-7215-0

VERSION NUMBER 01/26/26

Scripture quotations are from the ESV® Bible (The Holy Bible, English Standard Version®), © 2001 by Crossway, a publishing ministry of Good News Publishers. ESV Text Edition: 2025. The ESV text may not be quoted in any publication made available to the public by a Creative Commons license. The ESV may not be translated in whole or in part into any other language. Used by permission. All rights reserved.

All emphasis in Scripture quotations has been added by the author.

To Jesus, the Head of the church.

To Tiffany, my wife and best friend.

To every church leader called to build wisely.

Contents

Acknowledgments | ix

Introduction | xi

CHAPTER ONE *Foundations: An Overview of Corinth* | 1

CHAPTER TWO *Anchored in Grace: Leading from the Overflow of God's Past, Present, and Future Grace* | 8

CHAPTER THREE *Cruciform Leadership: Preaching the Cross in a World of Compromise* | 15

CHAPTER FOUR *Unveiling the Mystery: Leading Through the Spirit's Wisdom* | 23

CHAPTER FIVE *Building Wisely: Eternal Outcomes in God's Work* | 30

CHAPTER SIX *Correct, Imitate, Empower: Paul's Blueprint for the Church* | 37

CHAPTER SEVEN *Leaven in the Lump: Addressing Sin's Impact on the Church* | 44

CHAPTER EIGHT *Presenting Your Body to God: A Temple for the Lord* | 51

CHAPTER NINE *Sacrificial Leadership: A Foundation of Love* | 58

CONTENTS

CHAPTER TEN *The Key to Effective Ministry: Serving with Discipline and Purpose* | 66

CHAPTER ELEVEN *Supernatural Stewardship: Shepherding Spiritual Gifts with Wisdom* | 73

CHAPTER TWELVE *Every Member Matters: How the Holy Spirit Builds a Thriving Body* | 82

CHAPTER THIRTEEN *Leading with Love: The Heart of True Ministry* | 88

CHAPTER FOURTEEN *Order in the Spirit: Building Up, Not Tearing Down* | 99

CHAPTER FIFTEEN *Guarding the Message: Faithfulness to the Gospel in Ministry* | 105

CHAPTER SIXTEEN *Opportunities Versus Open Doors: How to Discern the Right Path in Ministry* | 114

Conclusion | 121

Bibliography | 123

Subject Index | 127

Scripture Index | 129

Acknowledgments

I am deeply grateful for the remarkable support system God has placed around me.

To my wife, Tiffany—God has used your steady love, your prayers, and your unwavering belief in me to strengthen every step of this journey. Your joy, wisdom, and faith have been a constant reminder of God's goodness in my life.

To my parents, David and Dawn—thank you for believing in me long before I ever began this work. Your love for the Lord, His Word, and His church—and the example you set in daily faithfulness—have profoundly shaped my life and ministry.

To my sister and brother-in-law, Jessica and Hayden—your unwavering support and prayers have meant more than you know.

To my in-laws, Andrew and Wendy, and Jill—thank you for cheering me on with such generosity of heart.

To my friends, Jonathan and Carl—your prayers have upheld me time and again.

To my mentors, Dr. Bekker, Reverend Grady, and Dr. Solomon—your wisdom, guidance, and example have shaped my life and my writing.

To my Reflection Church family—your prayers, encouragement, and shared love for Christ have been a continual source of strength.

Above all, I am thankful for the grace and empowering presence of the Lord Jesus. He led me into this work and sustained me through its completion—my strength, my shield, and my helper at every turn.

Introduction

My wife and I moved across the country to plant Reflection Church six months before the 2020 global pandemic. It was a dream fulfilled and a nightmare of unending difficulty. Health issues, infertility struggles, ministry betrayals, financial difficulty, and delayed outcomes were a few of the valleys we walked through. I remember telling my wife, "I don't know how much more God can break me." The Holy Spirit reminded me of A. W. Tozer's words, "It is doubtful whether God can bless a faithful man greatly until he has hurt him deeply."[1] Of course, God is not the author of harm, but He uses hardship to strip away self-reliance and draw us into deeper dependence on Him. Through it all, God was faithful. He was with us every step of the way. When it felt as though we could not take another step, God's zeal carried us and our church.

The myriad of challenges we faced kept bringing me back to 1 Corinthians. Of the sixty-six books of the Bible, it has been one of the most significant to my personal and ministry formation. In church leadership, we constantly face situations that demand a theological and practical response. First Corinthians offered me profound insights into the diverse situations I encountered. Our world needs less speculative, humanistic approaches and more biblically grounded counsel. A church leader cannot divorce Scripture's counsel from their own. All ministry and life endeavors must

---

1. Tozer, *Root of Righteousness*, 157.

be rooted in Scripture's proper interpretation and subsequent application. This is one of the primary differences between leadership and church leadership. Church leadership is tethered to Scripture's divine counsel. Therefore, church leaders must maintain a high and holy view of Scripture—its beauty, perfection, and authority. I frequently hold my Bible to my heart to remind me to treasure and cherish God's Word above everything else (Ps 119:11).

God does not seek leadership charisma. God seeks church leaders who are fascinated with Him and tremble at His Word (Isa 66:2). To that aim, each chapter surveys select passages from 1 Corinthians and their effects on church leaders, the church, and the culture. To do this effectively, we must locate 1 Corinthians in its proper context. One of my professors once said, "A text without a context is a con."[2] I earnestly pray that this book comforts, corrects, and inspires you in your life and ministry.

---

2. Mark Cartledge, in conversation with the author, Mar. 15, 2018.

CHAPTER ONE

Foundations
An Overview of Corinth

BACKGROUND

First Corinthians' historical, geographical, theological, political, and sociological landscape mirrors the diversity we experience in our world. It offers guidance for those willing to listen.[1] The apostle Paul was captivated by a call from the resurrected, glorified Jesus (Acts 9:15–16). He embarked on his second missionary journey around the Mediterranean Sea to metropolitan areas such as Troas, Philippi, Thessalonica, Berea, Athens, Corinth, and Ephesus (Acts 15:36—18:22). Driven by Jesus' mandate and the Holy Spirit's guidance (Acts 16:6–10), Paul faithfully proclaimed the gospel. He strategically ministered in growing metropolitan regions so diverse populations, including tourists and merchants, would hear the gospel. This approach enabled the gospel to spread around the known world.

As a religious scholar, an accomplished writer, a tentmaker, an itinerant preacher, a missionary, a mentor, and an apostolic

---

1. Thiselton, *First Epistle to the Corinthians*, 1–33.

leader (Acts 18:3, Phil 3:4–6), Paul was instrumental in transforming the religious landscape of the first-century world. His life and example in handling the Corinthians' diverse issues serve as a helpful guide for contemporary church leaders. Before surveying these examples, it is crucial to overview the city of Corinth, the church of Corinth, and the circumstances of Corinth.

The City of Corinth[2]

Corinth's geographical, political, and sociological norms are tied to Paul's Corinthian correspondence. Before its Roman control, Corinth was a thriving Greek city eclipsing the influence and prominence of Athens.[3] Rome strategically attacked Corinth in 146 BC as Rome ascended to geopolitical dominance.[4] By 44 BC Julius Caesar considered its value and rebuilt Corinth. Its population quickly rose to nearly eighty thousand people.[5] Corinth was an epicenter of commerce, athletic competition, and religious exploration by Paul's time.[6] Its strategic position on the isthmus created a land bridge that simplified economic exchange between Asia and Europe.[7] Sailors could drag their boats across the isthmus rather than sailing around Greece's dangerous southern coastline.[8]

Corinth specialized in manufacturing items like pottery, sculptures, lamps, and roof tiles.[9] This strengthened their economic ascent in the Greco-Roman world and created recreational opportunities. Take, for example, the Isthmian Games. They were only second in prestige to the Olympic Games and were hosted

---

2. Material in this chapter is derived, with revisions and expansions, from my previously published chapter on the subject (see Crisp, "Tale of Two Worlds," 177–82).
3. Blomberg, *1 Corinthians*, 18.
4. Blomberg, *1 Corinthians*, 18.
5. Blomberg, *1 Corinthians*, 19.
6. Pathrapankal, "From Areopagus to Corinth."
7. Thiselton, *First Epistle to the Corinthians*, 1.
8. Blomberg, *1 Corinthians*, 18.
9. Johnson, *1 Corinthians*, 15–16.

in Corinth every two years.[10] Additionally, Corinth provided a theater-style venue that seated eighteen thousand people and an additional concert area that held three thousand people.[11]

Corinth sported a multiethnic demography. The edict of Claudius, resulting in the expulsion of Jews from Rome because of their connection to Jesus, increased Jewish Corinthian inhabitants.[12] Jewish and Greco-Roman residents found Corinth a desirable home because of its economic success, athletic competitions, and connectedness to Rome. As a Roman city and colony, Corinthian citizens could vote and elect their officials annually.[13] Moreover, Corinthian citizens could own property and initiate adjudication for wrongdoing.[14]

Corinth's ethnic plurality created religious plurality. Corinthians worshiped gods within the vast Greek pantheon in many temples.[15] New Testament scholar Dr. Johnson offers this description: "Archaeological and literary evidence shows that Corinth had temples or sanctuaries devoted to the gods Aphrodite (two varieties), Isis and Serapis, Artemis, Dionysus, Poseidon, Apollo, Helius, Pelagrina, Necessity, Fates, Demeter, Maid, Zeus, Asklepius, Hermes, Athena and Hera Bunaea."[16] In addition to the Greek pantheon, Corinth also pledged its fidelity to the Roman imperial cult by worshiping the emperor himself. Relocated Christian Jews and the established Jewish community continued their allegiance to Jesus and Judaism.[17] Religious plurality defined Corinthian identity.

---

10. Blomberg, *1 Corinthians*, 19.
11. Blomberg, *1 Corinthians*, 19.
12. Thiselton, *First Epistle to the Corinthians*, 17.
13. Johnson, *1 Corinthians*, 15.
14. Johnson, *1 Corinthians*, 15–19.
15. Pathrapankal, "From Areopagus to Corinth."
16. Johnson, *1 Corinthians*, 17.
17. Pathrapankal, "From Areopagus to Corinth."

The Church of Corinth

Corinth's diversity and wealth appealed to the pagan world, but those with a Judeo-Christian worldview viewed the city as tainted "by the worship of idols, sexual immorality, and greed."[18] For the most part, Corinthian Christians did not experience Corinth's wealth. They were in the lower socioeconomic group.[19] Corinthian Christians were not, however, monolithic. First Corinthians indicates the Corinthian church ranged from wealthy individuals (1 Cor 11:17–22) to house servants (1 Cor 7:20–24). This wide income disparity unfortunately resulted in sinful classism (1 Cor 11:17–22).[20]

Corinth's spirituality cultivated an openness to the message of Jesus. However, its religious pluralism struggled with Christianity's exclusive claim. Many Corinthian converts came from pluralistic, idolatrous pasts, which required the Corinthians to maintain new societal parameters so they did not shame the gospel, revert to idolatrous living, or create stumbling blocks for fellow believers (1 Cor 8–10).[21]

Corinth's moral carelessness was known throughout Rome, earning them a specialized verb "that transliterates as 'to korinthianize,' meaning, 'to live an immoral lifestyle.'"[22] Moral laxity bled into the Christian community. They were engulfed in racial, sexual, and judicial problems. They also weaponized their spiritual gifts to demonstrate spiritual superiority (1 Cor 12–14). All issues considered, Dr. Engels provides a compelling case for the Corinthian church's significance despite its prevailing problems: "Corinth was a logical place to establish a strong Christian church, for its numerous trade connections would assure the rapid propagation of the new religion, and quite soon it came to dominate the other churches of the province."[23]

18. Ciampa and Rosner, *Corinthians*, 3.
19. Verbrugge, "1 Corinthians," 244.
20. Verbrugge, "1 Corinthians," 244.
21. Verbrugge, "1 Corinthians," 244.
22. Verbrugge, "1 Corinthians," 244.
23. Engels, *Roman Corinth*, 20.

The Circumstances of Corinth

The archeological finding of the Delphic letter of Claudius enabled biblical scholars to locate 1 Corinthians between AD 54 and 55.[24] During Paul's second missionary journey, he laid the apostolic foundation for the Corinthian church (1 Cor 1:2) and subsequently invested eighteen months building upon that foundation (Acts 18:1–18).[25] On his third missionary journey years later, Paul sent 1 Corinthians from Ephesus (1 Cor 16:8) and mentioned a previous noncanonical letter that had not produced the repentance he hoped for.[26]

Written and oral reports of sexual immorality, greed, and idolatry were situational reasons for Paul's correspondence (1 Cor 1:11, 16:17).[27] The categories of sexual immorality (1 Cor 5:1–13, 6:12–20, 7:1–40), greed (1 Cor 6:1–11), and idolatry (1 Cor 8–10) are part of the letter's purpose; however, "[1] peace within the church, [2] holiness in the world, and [3] fidelity to the gospel" better outline the letter's purpose.[28]

THEMES OF PEACE, HOLINESS, AND FIDELITY IN 1 CORINTHIANS

The most substantial contributions to the theme of peace are found in 1 Cor 1:11—4:21 and 1 Cor 8:1—11:1. Here, Paul addressed the divisive nature of the world's knowledge and wisdom versus God's wisdom and love.[29] Paul revisited this theme by addressing peace through unity in corporate worship practices (1 Cor 11:2–16), the Lord's Supper (1 Cor 11:17–34), and spiritual gifts (1 Cor 12:1—14:40).[30]

---

24. Thiselton, *First Epistle to the Corinthians*, 32.
25. Ciampa and Rosner, *Corinthians*, 2–3.
26. Ciampa and Rosner, *Corinthians*, 2–3.
27. Ciampa and Rosner, *Corinthians*, 2–3.
28. Thielman, *Theology*, 278.
29. Thielman, *Theology*, 278.
30. Witherington, *Conflict and Community*, 75–76.

Paul believed peace was not disconnected from holiness.[31] Holiness created parameters for Christian unity amid pagan immorality. The Corinthians' sexual promiscuity and immorality soiled the gospel's reputation to nonbelieving Corinthians (1 Cor 5:1–13, 6:12–20).[32] Furthermore, affluent Corinthian Christians relied on Roman litigation to settle civil disputes among believers. This made them look petty and misaligned from their claimed gospel message (1 Cor 6:1–11).[33] Idolatry was another issue many Corinthian Christians struggled with. By keeping their idolatrous practices, they shamed the gospel's exclusive requirement (1 Cor 10:1–22).[34] Finally, Paul instructed the Corinthian church to guard their partnerships in marriage and business because intermingling belief and unbelief would set them up for disaster (1 Cor 7:12–16).

Fidelity to the gospel message was imperative in pluralistic Corinth. Paul viewed bodily resurrection as nonnegotiable to the gospel message.[35] Although Greco-Roman culture provided different views about the separation of body and soul at death, Paul preached the future, bodily resurrection from the dead.[36] Paul said the Corinthians' efforts were in vain without the bodily resurrection, and their faith was dead (1 Cor 15:13–19, 58).

For these reasons, Paul's Corinthian correspondence is best viewed as an occasional letter bringing the Corinthian Christian community into unity through God's wisdom and love, holiness through sexual purity and public congruence, and fidelity to the gospel message through its exclusive claims.[37] This overview lays the historical and theological groundwork for practical applications for church leaders.

---

31. Thielman, *Theology*, 279.
32. Thielman, *Theology*, 291.
33. Thielman, *Theology*, 293–94.
34. Witherington, *Conflict and Community*, 76.
35. Thielman, *Theology*, 301.
36. Thielman, *Theology*, 303–5.
37. Thielman, *Theology*, 305.

KEY TAKEAWAYS

- Church leaders must ground their lives and ministries in Holy Scripture, revering and submitting to it.
- The challenges faced by Corinth's diverse, religiously pluralistic society mirror contemporary difficulties, offering insights into present ministry contexts.
- Corinth's sinful cultural influence seeped into the Corinthian church. Paul's strong biblical correction provides a paradigm for addressing cultural sinfulness in the contemporary church.

REFLECT

1. How does your view of Scripture influence your leadership methodology and approach?
2. What challenges does religious pluralism create for church leaders?
3. How can you cultivate peace and unity within your church so that it is a sign and witness to the unbelieving world?

CHAPTER TWO

Anchored in Grace
Leading from the Overflow of God's Past, Present, and Future Grace

> *I give thanks to my God always for you because of the grace of God that was given you in Christ Jesus, that in every way you were enriched in him in all speech and all knowledge—even as the testimony about Christ was confirmed among you—so that you are not lacking in any gift, as you wait for the revealing of our Lord Jesus Christ, who will sustain you to the end, guiltless in the day of our Lord Jesus Christ. God is faithful, by whom you were called into the fellowship of his Son, Jesus Christ our Lord.*
>
> — 1 Cor 1:4-9

INTRODUCTION

After addressing the scandalously behaved Corinthians as saints, the apostle Paul proved their conduct, although unacceptable and needing correction, did not change God's divine decree of their identity. Their primary identification was not *sinner*. Their sinful nature died in the watery grave of baptism (Rom 6:1–4). The Corinthians were reidentified as *saints* (ἅγιος) set apart *by* God *for* God. The Corinthian believers, and all those who belong to Christ, are God's holy people (1 Pet 2:9). Therefore, Paul did not engage in common flatteries that ancient writers used to build equity with their audience.[1] Instead, he praised God, urging them to focus on God, mentioning *Christ Jesus* eight times and *God* six times in the first nine verses.[2] It is God's grace the Corinthians needed. It is God's grace that church leaders need.

GOD'S GRACE IN THE PAST (VV. 4–6)

Paul emphasized God's grace as a past tense experience through the past tense phrase "that was given you" (τῇ δοθείσῃ ὑμῖν). This highlights God's prevenient grace, the grace that goes before, which God provides because of Christ's accomplishments on the cross (Titus 3:3–8). When the Corinthians were reidentified in Christ, they received what God purchased for them in and through Christ. Paul knew this because of his experience with God's grace. He wrote to the young pastoral leader, Timothy, "Though *formerly* I was a blasphemer, persecutor, and insolent opponent. But I *received* mercy because I had acted ignorantly in unbelief, and the grace of our Lord *overflowed* for me with the faith and love that are in Christ Jesus" (1 Tim 1:13–14). He told the young pastoral leader, Titus, "The grace of God *appeared*, bringing salvation for all people" (Titus 2:11). Paul plumbed the depths of his experience with God. That is what good church leaders do. They refuse to whitewash their life. God's grace bars that kind of pride: "For *by the grace given to me* I say to everyone among you not to think of himself more highly than he ought to think" (Rom 12:3). Church leaders share their successes and failures (Phil 3:4–11). They open the book of their life so others may read and learn (2 Cor 3:2–3).

---

1. Gardner, *1 Corinthians*, 55.
2. Gardner, *1 Corinthians*, 55.

Healthy transparency is the foundation of meaningful transformation within any group, especially God's church.[3] That is why you must become a herald of God's grace as the entry point for re-identification in Christ and the subsequent outcomes of internal transformation.

Paul explained to the Corinthians that God's grace caused *enrichment* (ἐπλουτίσθητε) in Christ. They were given riches in Christ Jesus.[4] These riches far surpass the materialistic possessions we often hear preached in this passage. They explain two specific forms of enrichment:

1. Enrichment *in all speech* (ἐν παντὶ λόγῳ)—describes the Corinthians' ability to express spiritual knowledge (1 Cor 1–2), to preach the gospel message (1 Cor 1:17, 9:16–23, 15:1–3), and to utilize the gift of tongues (1 Cor 12–14). God's grace-empowered speech differed from the Greco-Roman Sophists and philosophers. Why? Grace-empowered speech is not based on human intellect but on divine grace.[5] Church leaders understand God's gifts are from God's grace (*grace-gift*; χάρισμα).[6] This tempers the temptation toward pride and self-reliance, grounding church leaders in God's grace to empower their speech for His purposes.

2. Enrichment *in all knowledge* (πάσῃ γνώσει)—describes knowledge about spiritual matters and knowledge given by prophetic revelation.[7] Because of the public nature of speech gifts, they can cause pride. Church leaders rely on words to teach, preach, and counsel. It becomes easy to focus on our words above God's gracious empowerment. Unfortunately, this mindset permeates today's church. Preaching has often become an evaluated performance where gospel proclamation is exchanged for

---

3. Jiang and Men, "Creating an Engaged Workforce," 225–43.

4. Louw and Nida, s.v. "59.59 πλουτίζω," *Greek-English Lexicon*. Hereafter cited as L&N.

5. Gardner, *1 Corinthians*, 62.

6. Gardner, *1 Corinthians*, 62.

7. Ellingworth and Hatton, *Handbook*, 13.

conversations buoyed by props. Viewing speech as God's grace-gift helps curb this plague, keeping church leaders humble and dependent upon God's grace rather than prideful self-reliance.

Paul also thanked God for the Corinthians' verifiable (*confirmed*; ἐβεβαιώθη) reception of God's grace.[8] When you experience God's grace, it is obvious. No one wonders whether you experienced it or not because it changes you. Your belief and behavior align (Matt 3:8). Theological errors about grace distort this simple truth. Grace is not a message of misaligned living. Grace is a message of God's empowerment to overcome sin's ravages and experience Christ's riches.[9] Good church leaders do not abuse God's grace. They are changed by it and welcome others into its transforming power.

GOD'S GRACE IN THE PRESENT (V. 7)

Paul connected God's past-tense grace to God's present-tense provisions. God's grace ensured that the Corinthians did not lack any spiritual gift. Dr. Trail said this about the Corinthian church: "They have all that could be expected for a church on earth to have."[10] Although Paul corrected their misuse of spiritual gifts (1 Cor 12–14), he was grateful that God's grace supplied the needed gifts. God wants church leaders empowered by His gifts (2 Tim 1:6).

Here is the good news: God's present grace empowers church leaders to function at a higher level than they are naturally capable of. God does this through access to the nine spiritual gifts: (1) the utterance of wisdom, (2) the utterance of knowledge, (3) faith, (4) gifts of healings, (5) the working of miracles, (6) prophecy, (7) distinguishing of spirits, (8) various kinds of tongues, and (9) the interpretation of tongues (1 Cor 12:8–10). In short, God's grace-gifts enable church leaders to (1) have divine intelligence about situations, people, and circumstances, (2) speak God's message

---

8. L&N, s.v. "28.44 βεβαιόω; βεβαίωσις."
9. Gordon, *Grace Empowerment*, 10–25.
10. Trail, *Exegetical Summary*, 25.

with specificity, clarity, and power, and (3) believe for and see the impossible happen. We desperately need church leaders who are not fascinated with themselves but humbly rely upon God's gracious gifts.

Additionally, God's grace helped the Corinthians remain eager, expectant, and loyal as they awaited Jesus' return.[11] God's grace does not simply cover sins as we wait for Christ's return. God's grace trains us to renounce sin, live holy, and wait properly for His return (Titus 2:11–13). You have believed a false gospel if you believe giving your life to Christ, living in sin, and saying you are sorry is Christ's redemptive plan. God's grace transforms us by training us to renounce ungodliness (Titus 2:12). Church leaders mock God's grace when their lives are marked by unholiness and spiritual laziness. We honor His grace by holy, spiritually attentive living. This inspires congregants when they see their leader's spiritual faithfulness and intensity.[12] If you have grown spiritually lethargic, ask God for an outpouring of His grace in your life so you remain eager and faithful.

GOD'S GRACE IN THE FUTURE (VV. 8–9)

Paul told the Corinthians, God's grace will keep you until the *end* (τέλος). This term describes a person's endpoint or death. It is comforting to know when you die, God's grace meets you there. Each day until then, God's grace meets you here. Like the way God provided the Hebrews quail and manna each day (Exod 16), it is with God's grace. Perhaps that is why Jesus taught His disciples to pray, "Give us this day our daily bread" (Matt 6:11). Relying upon God's grace day by day helps church leaders not be overwhelmed. It dissipates anxiety that does not change outcomes (Matt 6:27). No matter the problems you face, be encouraged; God's grace will sustain you every single day until the *end* (τέλος).

---

11. Trail, *Exegetical Summary*, 26.
12. Kouzes and Posner, *Leadership Challenge*, 29–59.

When your life is *completed* (τέλος), the same grace that covered you day by day will keep you guiltless and blameless at the Great White Throne Judgment (Rev 20:11–15). Those in Christ will be secure against the judgment of hell.[13] Why? God has declared us righteous.[14] He has declared us clean. He has declared us forgiven. Your exceptional leadership skills will not grant you this future grace. You will experience it because of God's grace. That is why Paul prayed, "I give thanks to my God always for you because of the *grace of God* that was *given you in Christ Jesus*" (1 Cor 1:4). God's past-tense grace is a down payment of His future grace. That is why Paul said, "God is faithful" (1 Cor 1:9). God is trustworthy and reliable. Since He gave grace in the past and present, we can trust He will give grace in the future.[15] You do not need to be overwhelmed by the challenges and difficulties ahead. God's grace will ground you in the present and give you peace about the future. Do not be overwhelmed by church responsibilities. It belongs to Him, not you (Col 1:18, Eph 1:22–23). It is God's responsibility to build His church (Matt 16:18, Ps 127:1). It is God's zeal that accomplishes it (Isa 9:7). Enjoy laboring under the easy yoke of Jesus, not striving to build something great in your strength (Matt 18:20).

KEY TAKEAWAYS

- Church leaders lead from God's divine decree as saints rather than by their successes and failures.
- Church leaders must not hide their struggles but healthily and appropriately share how God's grace has transformed them.
- God's grace is not a license for compromised, sinful leadership. It is God's empowerment to live holy before God and His people.

---

13. Trail, *Exegetical Summary*, 27.
14. Trail, *Exegetical Summary*, 27.
15. L&N, s.v. "31.87 πιστός."

- Church leaders serve diligently and rely on God's grace as the church's builder and the leader's sustainer.

REFLECT

1. Record specific moments where God's grace met you in the past. Meditate upon them and allow them to encourage you.
2. How can you maintain transparency about your journey with God's grace without overemphasizing your struggles or achievements?
3. Based on God's past and present grace, actively lay down your anxieties, fears, and worries about the future and rely upon God's future grace.

CHAPTER THREE

Cruciform Leadership
Preaching the Cross in a World of Compromise

For the word of the cross is folly to those who are perishing, but to us who are being saved it is the power of God. For it is written, "I will destroy the wisdom of the wise, and the discernment of the discerning I will thwart." Where is the one who is wise? Where is the scribe? Where is the debater of this age? Has not God made foolish the wisdom of the world? For since, in the wisdom of God, the world did not know God through wisdom, it pleased God through the folly of what we preach to save those who believe. For Jews demand signs and Greeks seek wisdom, but we preach Christ crucified, a stumbling block to Jews and folly to Gentiles, but to those who are called, both Jews and Greeks, Christ the power of God and the wisdom of God. For the foolishness of God is wiser than men, and the weakness of God is stronger than men.

— 1 Cor 1:18–25

INTRODUCTION

The Corinthians struggled with divisions, boasting, arrogance, and cultural measurements. Their skewed view of wisdom and the crucified Christ disabled them from correctly understanding God and themselves.[1] Paul presented the crucified Christ as the antidote for fascination with and pursuit of worldly achievement. The message of the cross pierces contemporary understandings of greatness and a church leader's desire for success.

THE CROSS'S MESSAGE DIVIDES HUMANITY (V. 18)

Paul sought to dismantle the Corinthians' pride and self-reliance from their philosophical achievements. He did this by avoiding the philosophical approach of his day. Paul did not preach with human wisdom and eloquence because "the cross signals the end of human wisdom."[2] As difficult as this approach may seem for contemporary church leaders, this approach is rooted in the understanding that the message of the cross divides humanity into two groups:

1. *Those who are perishing* (τοῖς μὲν ἀπολλυμένοις μωρία ἐστίν)— The term *perishing* (ἀπολλυμένοις) describes one who is "ruined or destroyed."[3] The present tense nature of this verb describes the active, current process of a person's destruction. People who reject the cross's message are presently being destroyed but are not ultimately destroyed until the judgment seat of Christ. Thankfully, there is time for repentance as long as a person is alive. The bad news is that the cross's message is foolish to those perishing because it assaults the world's value of glory, power, and success.[4] That is why church leaders should never attempt to sanitize the cross's seeming

---

1. Witherington, *Conflict and Community*, 108.
2. Ciampa and Rosner, *Corinthians*, 90.
3. Ciampa and Rosner, *Corinthians*, 90–91.
4. Ciampa and Rosner, *Corinthians*, 91.

foolishness to those perishing. This seemingly foolish message is God's power unto salvation. If the message changes, it is stripped of its innate power that provides salvation (Rom 1:16). Additionally, preaching another gospel brings a curse upon the false preacher (Gal 1:8). Church leaders should never attempt to recontextualize the seeming foolishness of the cross.

2. *Those being saved* (τοῖς δὲ σῳζομένοις)—As in the case of *perishing, being saved* (σῳζομένοις) is a present tense verb describing a process of salvation for those trusting the cross's message. Those entrusting their life to the cross's message will also be saved on the last day. Notice that Paul did not contrast foolishness with wisdom. He contrasted foolishness and power. Paul reminded the Corinthians that the message of the cross is the revelation of God's power. Church leaders must remember that the cross's message is not merely a message of words but of power (1 Cor 4:20). It is not zingers from sermons that powerfully change lives. It is the cross that powerfully changes lives. When you see someone who trusts the message of the cross, your knee-jerk reaction is not, "Look how intelligent they are." Your knee-jerk response is, "Look how different they are." The cross's message transformed them from who they were (*perishing*; ἀπολλυμένοις) to who they are (*being saved*; σῳζομένοις).

Church leaders must not fall into the trap of trying to communicate a new, tolerable message but a true, transformative message. Do not measure the impact of your message or ministry by post-service stat sheets. Jesus' parable of the sower reveals that only one out of four soils receives the message rightly (Mark 4:1–20). Additionally, Jesus' parable shows that it takes time to see harvest from the one soil that rightly receives the message. Do not measure your ministry's effectiveness by immediate change. Though it seems offensive to the culture and distasteful to the hearer, faithfully preach the cross's message. That is the only power to transform lives. Its message gives piercing clarity in a culture clouded with ambiguity—those *perishing* (ἀπολλυμένοις) and those *being saved* (σῳζομένοις).

THE CROSS'S MESSAGE DESTROYS WORLDLY WISDOM (VV. 19-20)

To further expose Corinthian division, Paul described how the cross's message destroys worldly wisdom. To explain this, Paul quoted Isa 29:14, in which God pronounced judgment upon those who honored Him with their lips while their hearts were far from Him. Contextually, Isaiah prophesied against those who believed their message and manufactured rules about God made them more intelligent than God.[5] Isaiah foretold the coming destruction of that kind of thinking. God annihilated worldly wisdom with a crucified Messiah on a cross. This message is the furthest thing from worldly wisdom—the Davidic Warrior-King publicly executed by the empire His followers believed He would overthrow.[6]

The cross reveals that human wisdom that is not submitted to God's counsel is useless. God invalidates attempts to figure things out with our intellect.[7] Church leaders must receive this weighty warning. Guard your heart against human wisdom, training, metrics, and formation that instruct you to adopt "proven" methodologies that "work." It is not just about achieving outcomes. God cares about *how* we achieve outcomes. If you do not believe me, ask King David. He got a man killed by trying to achieve a great result with the wrong method (2 Sam 6:1-11). Be careful not to exchange divine wisdom for human wisdom, deceiving yourself and convincing yourself that God wants it done "that way." Remember, everyone viewed Jesus as a complete and total failure—a crucified Messiah cursed by God on a tree (Deut 21:23). Jesus was not concerned with the crowd's perception but with faithfulness to His Father. He went to the cross in obedience and left the results

---

5. Verbrugge, "1 Corinthians," 269.
6. Verbrugge, "1 Corinthians," 269.
7. Trail, *Exegetical Summary*, 48.

to His Father. God vindicated Jesus by raising Him from the dead, giving Him a name above every name, destroying the powers of darkness, and providing salvation for all who believe (Acts 2:24, Rom 1:16, Phil 2:9, Col 2:15). Ministry results are not your job. Faithfulness is your job. If you faithfully communicate the cross's message, God will honor your ministry whether you have five people or five thousand. Being known on earth is not the goal. Being known in heaven is. Faithfulness to the cross's message ensures you are known in heaven (Luke 16:10, 2 Tim 4:2). Paul challenged three groups who relied on worldly wisdom:

1. *The wise person* (σοφός)—likely Greek Sophists and Platonic philosophers who scoffed at a crucified Christ.

2. *The scribe* (γραμματεύς)—likely Jewish persons well-versed in the law who scoffed at the thought of a crucified Christ.

3. *The debater* (συζητητής) *of this age*—likely the public who enjoyed philosophical debate and discussion for its own sake. Such debate was depicted at the Areopagus, where people were "always . . . learning but never arriv[ing] at a knowledge of the truth" (2 Tim 3:7, Acts 17:19–34).

The world attempts to amass wisdom without the lens of the crucified Christ. If worldly wisdom could lead people to God, the wise person, the scribe, and the debater would discover Him. However, we do not know God through human wisdom but through divine revelation in the crucified Christ.[8] Be careful not to become enamored with human wisdom. The crucified Christ is the only lens we should look through as we seek understanding. Any answer, methodology, or ministry endeavor without that lens cannot be trusted.

THE CROSS'S MESSAGE MUST BE PREACHED (VV. 21–25)

The world does not know God through human wisdom. God has chosen the preaching of the cross's message to reveal Himself. As

8. Witherington, *Conflict and Community*, 112.

a church leader, never feel that preaching is antiquated or unimportant. It is God's chosen delivery system for divine revelation and salvation. I understand the sentiment behind the popular quote, "Preach the gospel at all times. If necessary, use words." It isn't wholly biblical, though. Paul explained that "it pleased God through the folly of *what we preach* to save those who believe" (1 Cor 1:21). Church leaders must preach the cross's message. With churches increasingly removing the cross's offense by eliminating crosses from their buildings, stages, and sermons, God is seeking a revival of preaching the cross.

You are in good company if you feel the cross's message is unpopular. Paul felt that way, too. The Jews expected a victorious king who would restore Israel's grandeur.[9] To the Jews, the cross's message was like us hearing, "Let's celebrate! The holiday is canceled."[10] The Greeks sought to attain divine knowledge through speculative philosophy.[11] They could not grasp the concept of a suffering God.[12] The cross's message was not popular, yet Paul preached it faithfully.

He learned from his mistakes. Many adopt Paul's methodology found in Athens's Areopagus, championing it as the end-all-be-all method for preaching (Acts 17:22–34). However, Paul abandoned this methodology based on philosophical debate. He told the Corinthians,

> And I, when I came to you, brothers, did not come proclaiming to you the testimony of God with *lofty speech or wisdom*. For I decided to *know nothing* among you except Jesus Christ and him crucified. And I was with you *in weakness and in fear and much trembling*, and *my speech and my message were not in plausible words of wisdom*, but in demonstration of the Spirit and of power, so that *your faith might not rest in the wisdom of men* but in the power of God. (1 Cor 2:1–5)

9. Ciampa and Rosner, *Corinthians*, 99–100.
10. Ciampa and Rosner, *Corinthians*, 99.
11. Blomberg, *1 Corinthians*, 53.
12. Blomberg, *1 Corinthians*, 53.

Philosophical methodologies should never eclipse a church leader's humble dependence on preaching the cross's message.

When we preach the cross's message, it does not matter if you are Jew or Greek, intelligent or unintelligent, rich or poor. It pierces the heart and reveals God's power and wisdom (Acts 2:37).[13] The cross's message is enough. The crucified Christ is enough. We do not need additional bells and whistles. Our job is "not to create a persuasive message at all, but to convey effectively the already articulated message of another."[14] This countercultural mindset will be viewed as simple, narrow-minded, and without thought. Dr. Blomberg offers this encouragement to church leaders:

> Secular and liberally minded religious scholars as well as self-taught philosophers and gurus . . . tolerate every bizarre and immoral ideology conceivable but refuse to include born-again Christians in their antidiscrimination campaigns. . . . We should avoid the constant peril of trying to imitate secular standards of wisdom . . . [as it leads to] spiritual impotence apart from the crucified Christ working through us.[15]

Dr. Murphy-O'Conner adds,

> Any attempt to make the gospel palatable by bringing it into line with the tastes of those to whom it is preached distorts it, because in this case the criterion is made the expectations of *fallen* humanity. In so doing, it loses its power.[16]

We must be okay with people mocking us for our simple conclusion. Why? "The foolishness of God is wiser than men, and the weakness of God is stronger than men" (1 Cor 1:25). As church leaders, we must cling to the cross's message and never be ashamed (Luke 9:26, Rom 1:16). Only the cross's message produces lasting life transformation.

---

13. Blomberg, *1 Corinthians*, 53.
14. Ciampa and Rosner, *Corinthians*, 97.
15. Blomberg, *1 Corinthians*, 60.
16. Quoted in Blomberg, *1 Corinthians*, 56; emphasis original.

KEY TAKEAWAYS

- People's eternal status is determined by how they respond to the cross's message.
- Church leaders must resist the pull to make the cross's message more palatable and must trust the cross's message is God's power to transform lives.
- Ministry is more than measuring metrics. It is about being faithful to God. The results and outcomes belong to Him anyway.
- We cannot achieve God's transforming work through human strategies but through the cross's message.

REFLECT

1. How do you measure ministry success? Is it primarily based on visible results like financial and numerical growth? Or is it based on faithfulness to God's directives?

2. How can I ensure my ministry remains centered on the crucified Christ rather than contemporary philosophies, trends, or "bells and whistles"?

3. How often do I pray for God's power and wisdom in my preaching and ministry, trusting that His "foolishness" is greater than human wisdom?

CHAPTER FOUR

Unveiling the Mystery
Leading Through the Spirit's Wisdom

> *Yet among the mature we do impart wisdom, although it is not a wisdom of this age or of the rulers of this age, who are doomed to pass away. But we impart a secret and hidden wisdom of God, which God decreed before the ages for our glory. None of the rulers of this age understood this, for if they had, they would not have crucified the Lord of glory. But, as it is written, "What no eye has seen, nor ear heard, nor the heart of man imagined, what God has prepared for those who love him"—these things God has revealed to us through the Spirit. For the Spirit searches everything, even the depths of God. For who knows a person's thoughts except the spirit of that person, which is in him? So also no one comprehends the thoughts of God except the Spirit of God. Now we have received not the spirit of the world, but the Spirit who is from God, that we might understand the things freely given us by God. And we impart this in words not taught by human wisdom but taught by the Spirit, interpreting spiritual truths to those who are spiritual. The natural person does not accept the things of the Spirit of God, for they are folly to him, and he is not able to understand them because they are*

spiritually discerned. The spiritual person judges all things, but is himself to be judged by no one. "For who has understood the mind of the Lord so as to instruct him?" But we have the mind of Christ.

— 1 Cor 2:6–16

INTRODUCTION

In this passage, Paul used contrasts to describe the mysteries of divine revelation. He reminded the Corinthians that divine wisdom is only experienced through the Holy Spirit's revelation. They could not use worldly wisdom to receive God's thoughts and plans. This message offers a healthy corrective to church leaders trying to figure everything out through their own lens, experience, and methodological approach. We must rely upon the Holy Spirit.

GOD'S WISDOM WRAPPED IN MYSTERY (VV. 6–8)

Paul informed the Corinthians, who were fascinated with philosophical ideations and debates, that wisdom is imparted to *mature* (τέλειος) believers. Who are *mature* (τέλειος) believers? Those who understand and conform to the cross's message. The length of one's relationship with Jesus does not define spiritual maturity. Maturity is determined by valuing the cross's message above worldly wisdom. The immature despised Paul's preaching of the cross as over-simplistic and lacking wisdom.[1] Ironically enough, the Corinthians, who viewed themselves as mature, were immature.[2] This presents a sobering warning for church leaders. You can identify yourself wrongly. You can view your length of service to God as a benchmark for maturity rather than your view and value of His message. May we never overestimate our maturity but humbly

---

1. Trail, *Exegetical Summary*, 84.
2. Barry et al., *Faithlife Study Bible*, 1 Cor 2:6.

view ourselves as people constantly undergoing conformity to the crucified Christ (Rom 8:29, 12:3, Gal 2:20).

Let me clarify something. The secret mystery imparted to the mature is not cultish knowledge that requires fifteen years to grasp. Paul referenced this *mystery* (μυστήριον) in his writings as the gospel message once hidden but now revealed. The reason many religious leaders did not grasp the crucified Messiah is because God wrapped it in mystery.[3] That is why Paul wrote the following:

- Rom 16:25–26—"According to the revelation of the *mystery* that was kept secret for long ages but has now been disclosed and through the prophetic writings has been made known to all nations, according to the command of the eternal God."
- Col 1:25–26—"The *mystery* hidden for ages and generations but now revealed to his saints."
- Eph 3:4–6—"When you read this, you can perceive my insight into the *mystery* of Christ, which was not made known to the sons of men in other generations as it has now been revealed to his holy apostles and prophets by the Spirit. This *mystery* is that the Gentiles are fellow heirs, members of the same body, and partakers of the promise in Christ Jesus through the gospel."

This mystery was decreed and determined by God's divine wisdom and sovereignty. That is why John said, "The Lamb [was] slain from the foundation of the world" (Rev 13:8). God carried out this divinely planned mystery, so we share in the benefits of Jesus' sacrifice now and forever.[4] The rulers of this age did not comprehend God's mystery. If they had, they would not have crucified Jesus. Who are the "rulers of this age"? These rulers are wicked human rulers and the cosmic, demonic spirits behind them.[5] By crucifying Jesus, they staged their own defeat.[6] Although the general plan of

---

3. Blomberg, *1 Corinthians*, 63–64.
4. Trail, *Exegetical Summary*, 88.
5. Ciampa and Rosner, *Corinthians*, 125.
6. Verbrugge, "1 Corinthians," 277.

Satan being crushed by the woman's seed was revealed in Gen 3:15 (i.e., the *protoevangelium*), the specifics were not revealed. Only God had that information.[7] Until then, it was a mystery—secret wisdom kept hidden. Because of this, Christ "disarmed the rulers and authorities and put them to open shame, by triumphing over them in him" (Col 2:15). Christ eternally vanquished the rulers of this age by His death on the cross.[8] Church leaders must treasure this secret wisdom above worldly wisdom. After all, it is the only message that produces freedom, healing, deliverance, salvation, and transformation.

THE UNVEILING OF GOD'S MYSTERY (VV. 9-16)

We must consider, however, how God reveals this mystery. To explain this, Paul loosely quoted Isa 64:4: "What no eye has seen, nor ear heard, nor the heart of man imagined, what God has prepared for those who love him" (1 Cor 2:9). The context of Isa 64:4 is that wisdom and knowledge are not the primary way to understand God and His saving work. Those who receive revelation do not receive it because they are intelligent. They receive it because they love God. Their love for God opens them to the mysteries of God's Spirit.[9] Put simply, people cannot understand divine revelation through human means. Those who love God can only grasp it by the Spirit.[10]

The Holy Spirit actively searches, hovers, and broods over the depths of God. He knows the Father's attributes, plans, and desires.[11] The Holy Spirit knows God better than anyone. He *searches* (ἐραυνᾷ) God to reveal what He finds to us.[12] To clarify this, Paul used a human analogy about the nature of human thoughts. Only the person thinking a thought knows it since they have not yet

---

7. Witherington, *Conflict and Community*, 127.
8. Verbrugge, "1 Corinthians," 277.
9. Ciampa and Rosner, *Corinthians*, 128.
10. Barry et al., *Faithlife Study Bible*, 1 Cor 2:9.
11. Trail, *Exegetical Summary*, 93.
12. Arndt et al., s.v. "ἐραυνάω," *Greek-English Lexicon*. Hereafter cited as BDAG.

communicated that thought to another. The same is true of God. He has many thoughts about us, more numerous than the sand (Ps 139:17–18). We access those thoughts, plans, and desires by the Holy Spirit's revelation.

Worldly wisdom cannot reveal spiritual mysteries, although it tries to comprehend, compute, reason, and understand through natural means. The *spirit of the world*, like the *rulers of the world*, alludes to both the pride and independence of the world's wisdom and the nefarious influence of demonic spirits behind it. That is why the natural person who does not love God cannot perceive these mysteries. They cannot because they are not naturally discerned. Church leaders must abandon approaches that rely solely on wooing the natural mind. Even if you have fifteen PhDs, you cannot receive spiritual revelation solely on that basis. Spiritual revelation is not naturally discerned. It is spiritually discerned. It is not earned by years of service, intellectual status, or financial achievement. It is freely given because of Christ's finished accomplishment on the cross.

I'll never forget my frustration of trying to understand Scripture when I was eight. I asked my dad, "Why can't I understand Scripture even though I understand other books?" He responded, "It is not a natural book. It is a spiritual book. Have you asked the Holy Spirit to help you?" I hesitantly replied, "No." He said, "Go. Try that, and let's talk." After I prayed and asked the Holy Spirit to help me, divine revelation was given. I could understand! This is what church leaders must teach congregants. Yes, there are proper interpretive approaches. Yes, you need to understand the context. However, you cannot think your way into divine revelation. You receive it by the Holy Spirit (John 14:26, 1 John 2:27). New Testament scholar Dr. Gardner said, "These things have been revealed by God's Spirit, who comes from God to show Christians all that God has done for them and given them. It is grace from start to finish, something that this verse tells us the Spirit helps us 'know.'"[13]

Paul offered a question from Isa 40:13, "For who has understood the mind of the Lord so as to instruct him?" (1 Cor 2:16).

---

13. Gardner, *1 Corinthians*, 145–46.

He answered the question in this passage's context. Since the Spirit is freely given to those who accept the *mystery* (μυστήριον) of the crucified Christ, and the Holy Spirit reveals God's mysteries to them, they now have the mind of Christ. This mind can receive God's mysteries, wisdom, and thoughts—access to spiritual information and divine wisdom revealed by the Spirit.[14] If our goal as church leaders is to align people with God's plan, we cannot do that without the mind of Christ, which is tuned to God's mysteries, wisdom, and thoughts.[15] We cannot rely upon assimilation and discipleship tracks as the means of revelation. Those structural forms assist spiritual transformation, but only the Holy Spirit knows the growth track of His sheep. We must rely on His guidance for each person's growth and development. That is what a good church leader does. The Holy Spirit guides their path and those He has entrusted to them.

As Paul grasped this revelation, he praised God, "Oh, the depth of the riches and wisdom and knowledge of God! How unsearchable are his judgments and how inscrutable his ways! . . . For from him and through him and to him are all things. To him be glory forever. Amen" (Rom 11:33, 36). May we have this same gratitude for the Holy Spirit's revelation of divine mysteries.

KEY TAKEAWAYS

- Church leaders understand true wisdom comes from God, not human intellect that does not produce spiritual transformation.
- A church leader's maturity is based on understanding and applying the cross's message, not their accolades and achievements.
- Spiritual truths are only grasped by the Holy Spirit's revelation, not by human intellect and understanding.

---

14. Trail, *Exegetical Summary*, 105.
15. Blackaby and Blackaby, *Spiritual Leadership*, 31–50.

- Effective leadership requires receiving the mind of Christ and allowing the Holy Spirit to lead and guide a leader's thoughts and actions.

REFLECT

1. In what areas of my leadership am I tempted to rely on experience and methodology above the Holy Spirit's guidance?
2. How do I ensure that I rely upon spiritual revelation above natural revelation for my teaching and leading?
3. How can I balance helpful church structures and reliance upon the Holy Spirit's growth process?

CHAPTER FIVE

Building Wisely
Eternal Outcomes in God's Work

What then is Apollos? What is Paul? Servants through whom you believed, as the Lord assigned to each. I planted, Apollos watered, but God gave the growth. So neither he who plants nor he who waters is anything, but only God who gives the growth. He who plants and he who waters are one, and each will receive his wages according to his labor. For we are God's fellow workers. You are God's field, God's building. According to the grace of God given to me, like a skilled master builder I laid a foundation, and someone else is building upon it. Let each one take care how he builds upon it. For no one can lay a foundation other than that which is laid, which is Jesus Christ. Now if anyone builds on the foundation with gold, silver, precious stones, wood, hay, straw—each one's work will become manifest, for the Day will disclose it, because it will be revealed by fire, and the fire will test what sort of work each one has done. If the work that anyone has built on the foundation survives, he will receive a reward. If anyone's work is burned up, he will suffer loss, though he himself will be saved, but only as through fire.

— 1 Cor 3:5–15

INTRODUCTION

In Paul's discussion about divine wisdom and the Holy Spirit's revelation of divine mystery, Paul addressed the Corinthian church's divisions. Paul made clear there was no room for rivalry, competition, and division because the church is God's field, building, and harvest. Paul encouraged the Corinthians to shift their worldly understanding of competition against each other to a collaborative understanding of laboring together with God. Each person and church has unique gifts and anointings for the sake of the world. We must carefully tend to our co-laboring so that we do not build something God will burn up.

ONE PURPOSE (VV. 5-8)

Paul exposed Corinthian divisions with a humbling line of questioning. *What am I? What is Apollos?* The Corinthians revealed their spiritual immaturity by their treatment of one spiritual leader over another. Paul and Apollos were not God. The Corinthians' inappropriate exaltation of one leader over the other created sectarianism as they disregarded God's valid messengers because of their style, preference, and appearance. These cults of personality were exhibited by the Sophists' earthly wisdom, not Christ's spiritual wisdom. Unsurprisingly, sectarianism permeates today's church. Some churchgoers will not attend if their preferred preacher is not preaching. This is earthly wisdom based on favorites rather than spiritual wisdom based on hunger for God's Word. There is nothing wrong with having a preferred preacher. However, disregarding churches or ministries that are not yours because they are not yours is sinful and spiritually unwise.

What are Paul and Apollos, and any church leader for that matter? God's *servants* (διάκονος). Paul did not weaponize his apostolic authority. He came as God's humble servant. Paul and Apollos co-labored to make this dynamic church flourish. Perhaps the most excellent antidote to competitive, earthly wisdom is the simple theology of servitude—not just information or revelation but actualization. Paul actively modeled Christ's example as the chief διάκονος (Mark 10:45, Phil 2:5–8). What if our mindset shifted from how we are growing, building, and expanding to how I am serving God and His people, modeling Christ, and being faithful to His call? God is calling for a cataclysmic shift in church leaders from chief executive officer (CEO) to chief διάκονος (*servant*) officer (CDO).

To further illustrate their singular purpose, Paul employed an agricultural metaphor. "I planted, Apollos watered, but God gave the growth" (1 Cor 3:6). As the apostolic founder, Paul planted. As a gifted teacher of the Scriptures, Apollos watered. But God grew the Corinthian church. The Corinthians grew under Paul and Apollos's *service* (διάκονος), but God was the one growing them, not Paul and Apollos. Jesus taught this same message with the parable of the seed growing: "And he said, 'The kingdom of God is as if a man should scatter seed on the ground. He sleeps and rises night and day, and the seed sprouts and grows; he knows not how'" (Mark 4:26–27). Paul's point was that God is the one the Corinthians should focus on. Likewise, when congregants gather, the focus should not be on who is singing or preaching. The focus should be on God's goodness, power, glory, and beauty. God grows people and His church.[1]

The one who plants and the one who waters are one. They share the same purpose. They co-labor diversely to see the growth that only God brings. They partner together with God. Dr. Carson offers a helpful analogy:

> It is the project as a whole that is important, and, implicitly, it is foolish to focus all praise on just one of the builders who has contributed.[2]

Church leaders need each other. We need apostolically gifted leaders who plant and start things. We need pastorally gifted leaders who water and tend things. We need prophetically gifted people who confront the issues of our day and herald God's response to them. We need evangelistically gifted people who ignite passion for

---

1. Barry et al., *Faithlife Study Bible*, 1 Cor 3:6.
2. Carson, *Cross and Christian Ministry*, 78.

Christ's Commission. We need gifted teachers who carefully teach the Scriptures. All these divine gifts share a singular purpose—planting and watering so that God brings growth (Eph 4:11–16).

ONE BUILDING (VV. 9–11)

Paul shifted from an agricultural metaphor (God's field) to an architectural one (God's building).[3] The Corinthians said they belong to either Apollos or to Paul. No matter how important an individual is in our journey with Jesus, we do not belong to them. We belong to God. We are God's building. Paul said it this way to the Ephesian church, "You are fellow citizens with the saints and members of the household of God, built on the foundation of the apostles and prophets, Christ Jesus himself being the cornerstone, in whom the whole structure, being joined together, grows into a holy temple in the Lord. In him you also are being built together into a dwelling place for God by the Spirit" (Eph 2:19–22). God graced Paul to co-labor with Apollos and ultimately with God to skillfully build the Corinthian church. He laid the foundation like a *skilled master builder* (ἀρχιτέκτων). God graced Paul for Corinth and graces church leaders with dreams and visions for local churches.

In 2017–2018, I received two prophetic words about God seeing me as an ecclesial architect. In 2019, God called my wife and me to Oklahoma City to plant and pastor Reflection Church. This was four months before the 2020 global pandemic. There were moments I did not see a path forward. There were times when finances seemed impossible. Seeing eight people in the building felt like a miracle. God gave us divine wisdom, grace, and provision during these times. When the dream seemed all but dead, God's grace abounded. I am living proof that God's dream in us is carried out by God's grace upon us.

Yet, Paul made clear the focus should not be on what is being built but the foundation upon which it is built. Without the

---

3. Verbrugge, "1 Corinthians," 284.

foundation of Christ, there is no meaningful structure. Without Christ, there is no church. We can have beautiful buildings, stellar teams, and extraordinary strategies, plans, and goals. Without Christ, it is all pointless. The church is His building. He is the foundation. He is the head of the body (Eph 5:23). He is Alpha and Omega (Rev 22:13). He is everlasting to everlasting (Ps 90:1). He fills all in all (Eph 1:23). The church is about Him. There is no other foundation. Church leaders who build on another foundation are not building a church. They are building upon the dismantled wisdom of the world. It may be a building, but God's glory has departed (1 Sam 4:21). We only partner with God's building by building on His foundation. Imagine having a contractor lay a foundation, and then the construction workers build on the grass next to the foundation. Do not be deceived in this hour. There is only one foundation. It is not success. It is not achievement. It is not growth; growth is God's job. It is Jesus Christ alone.

ONE OF TWO OUTCOMES (VV. 12–15)

Paul warned Corinth and church leaders throughout the ages of God's seriousness about His building. To emphasize significant contrast, Paul presented six building materials in two groupings: (1) gold, silver, and precious stones, and (2) wood, hay, and straw. What is the difference between the two groups? The first can withstand God's judging fire. The second cannot. What we build and how we build is either gold, silver, and precious stones or wood, hay, and straw. There is no in-between.

Perhaps the most terrifying thought is that a church leader could spend their whole life thinking they are building on the foundation of Christ, only to discover their life's work has gone up in God's flames. If you rely purely on human wisdom, God will burn up your life's work. Human wisdom, which relies more on techniques, skills, marketing, and consulting, is wood, hay, and straw. Pure, humble *service* (διάκονος) through the preaching of and reliance upon the cross's message will produce a building of gold, silver, and precious stones. Church leadership is serious. It is not some vocational game. It is not an additional activity for your week.[4] God loves you. God loves His building. God has prescribed the right materials and the proper foundation.

Which building materials we choose produces one of two eternal outcomes: (1) a reward or (2) a reproach. Jesus taught about the reward in Luke 19. Jesus multiplied the minas of the faithful servants in the age to come for increased praise to God, increased responsibility, and increased crowns to cast at Jesus' feet. This reward is not salvation but the reward of faithful building. These faithful servants of God will receive the reward of oversight and responsibility in the age to come based on how they build now. The second outcome is sobering. It does not impact salvation. Works do not save us anyway. It does, however, deal with eternal consequences. It would be devastating to watch God burn the building you built for Him while He saves you from your burning building.[5] May we put down the wood, hay, and stubble of human strategy and reliance and stand upon the divine wisdom and revelation of Jesus Christ, and Him crucified. In the words of the famous hymn, "On Christ the solid rock I stand. All other ground is sinking sand. All other ground is sinking sand."[6]

KEY TAKEAWAYS

- Church leaders are not competing against each other. We serve God and those He has entrusted to us.
- We need other church leaders. Diverse giftings enable us to collaborate and accomplish more.
- Church leaders must abandon the CEO model to a service model where success is measured by faithfulness to God and His people rather than earthly measurable outcomes.

---

4. Verbrugge, "1 Corinthians," 285–86.
5. Blomberg, *1 Corinthians*, 74–75.
6. From Edward Mote's "My Hope Is Built on Nothing Less" (1834).

- Ministry based on human wisdom and worldly strategies instead of Christ's wisdom does not please God. It will not stand before Him.

REFLECT

1. How can you contribute to fostering unity and collaboration within your church?
2. What steps can you take to shift your focus from personal success to faithful service?
3. What materials are you using to build your life and ministry? How can you discern if they are aligned with God's eternal purposes?

CHAPTER SIX

Correct, Imitate, Empower
Paul's Blueprint for the Church

I do not write these things to make you ashamed, but to admonish you as my beloved children. For though you have countless guides in Christ, you do not have many fathers. For I became your father in Christ Jesus through the gospel. I urge you, then, be imitators of me. That is why I sent you Timothy, my beloved and faithful child in the Lord, to remind you of my ways in Christ, as I teach them everywhere in every church. Some are arrogant, as though I were not coming to you. But I will come to you soon, if the Lord wills, and I will find out not the talk of these arrogant people but their power. For the kingdom of God does not consist in talk but in power. What do you wish? Shall I come to you with a rod, or with love in a spirit of gentleness?

— 1 Cor 4:14–21

INTRODUCTION

At this point in Paul's letter, he appealed to the Corinthians as their founder, spiritual father, and first gospel preacher. Utilizing this unique relationship, Paul admonished them to be transformed. He desperately wanted them to move away from their prideful arrogance unto Christ's wisdom and humility.[1] The apostle Paul's exhortation offers church leaders a paradigm for admonishing and correcting issues within the church.

WE NEED CORRECTION (V. 14)

Paul did not correct the Corinthians to embarrass, shame, or disgrace them. He addressed them as brothers and sisters five times in the first four chapters. If his goal was shame, he would not have used familial language. The Greek term used, *admonish* (νουθετέω), generally indicates parental instruction.[2] The Corinthians were Paul's *beloved children*. What do loving fathers do? They *admonish* (νουθετέω) their children. Paul warned them that their behaviors, actions, attitudes, and mindsets produced divisions, sexual immorality, lawsuits, and a myriad of other issues. Their nonsensical behavior was worse than unbelievers. They needed correction.

Paul's criticism and admonishment of their pride and sectarianism was not out of shame but out of love.[3] Our current culture cannot grasp this differentiation. Correction or warning is not hatred, condemnation, or shame. It is love for those practicing destructive ways. How much would you have to hate someone to hide the truth from them? Church leaders must learn how to be corrected and how to issue correction. Jesus said it this way: "And blessed is the one who is not *offended* by me" (Matt 11:6). Paul said it this way to Timothy: "All Scripture is breathed out by God and profitable for teaching, for *reproof*, for *correction*, and for training in righteousness" (2 Tim 3:16). Proverbs 12:1 says this: "Whoever

---

1. Barry et al., *Faithlife Study Bible*, 1 Cor 4:14–21.
2. Trail, *Exegetical Summary*, 180.
3. Trail, *Exegetical Summary*, 180.

loves *discipline* loves knowledge, but he who hates *reproof* is stupid." Hebrews 12:11 says, "For the moment all *discipline* seems painful rather than pleasant, but later it yields the peaceful fruit of righteousness to those who have been trained by it." We must grow up in the Spirit and learn how to receive correction. Too many church leaders and churchgoers call correction church hurt. The moment correction is issued, they leave and blame the church. Now is the time to value warning, exhortation, and correction.

Our church's leaders were prayerfully considering a transition to a new property, which would have removed our $175,000 remaining mortgage and given us over $1,000,000 cash to renovate an existing church double the size. As a visionary and dreamer, I got excited. One morning, my phone buzzed early with an alert. It was a mentor of mine with a prophetic word. I was fired up! What might the Lord want to say to us? The message read, "I was praying for you and got this verse from Proverbs 19:2, 'Being excited about something is not enough. You must also know what you are doing. Don't rush into something, or you might do it wrong.'" Ouch. This did not feel good. I did not particularly like the word. But I prayerfully weighed it. It was God's word to me. I let that word correct me. I let it sink into my heart. Correction is not always fun. It is needed.

The Corinthians did not want to be publicly demeaned in their status-focused world. Paul pastorally and fatherly corrected them in love. May we all be mature enough to receive warning, exhortation, admonition, and correction.[4]

WE NEED RELATIONAL DISCIPLESHIP (VV. 15-17)

Though the Corinthians had many guides, they did not have many fathers. The term *guide* (παιδαγωγός) describes well-known figures in Greco-Roman society. A pedagogue would take a son to their tutor and help them with lessons when they came home.

---

4. Gardner, *1 Corinthians*, 213.

They were a significant part of the child's life, but they were not the father.[5] A pedagogue's role ended when the son became an adult. The father's role never ends. Paul did not use the term *guide* (παιδαγωγός) pejoratively. The Corinthians needed guides, guardians, and teachers. They had Apollos, Peter, their current leaders, and others who gave necessary instruction and guidance. They tutored them in the faith. However, Paul was their father in the faith. He was present for their spiritual birth. He nursed them with the pure milk of God's Word. He walked them through deliverance from false worship. As a father, he came to offer the discipline only a father could offer.

Our contemporary Christian circles love instructors, but we often distance ourselves from relational discipleship. We love podcasts, reels, TV preachers, books, sermons, and spiritual growth resources. We don't like accountability. Yes, some leaders have weaponized their power. However, bad spiritual leaders do not negate the need for spiritual leadership and discipleship. A lousy church experience does not mean all churches are bad. We desperately need discipleship, not just information dispensers.

The aim of relational discipleship is not just correction but imitation. A spiritual father or mother is not a lecturer, although they teach. Their aim is imitation. The best disciples are made by imitating what they see, not just replicating what they hear. Jesus was clear in the Great Commission that "teaching them *to obey* all I have commanded" is critical to disciple-making (Matt 28:18–20). Jesus also "appointed twelve (whom he also named apostles) so that they might *be with him* and he might send them out to preach and have authority to cast out demons" (Mark 3:14–15). Proximity is critical to relational discipleship. Proximity enables formation by seeing how spiritual fathers and mothers respond, serve, pray, study, and handle adversity. If this were not the case, Paul would not have said to the Corinthians, "Be imitators of me, as I am of Christ" (1 Cor 11:1). Dr. Soards notes that in antiquity,

---

5. Verbrugge, "1 Corinthians," 297.

children and disciples internalized the values, thoughts, and behaviors of their role models so that they became very much like them.[6]

Paul exemplified this model with his spiritual son, Timothy. When Paul was not able to come to Corinth, he sent Timothy. Why? Timothy replicated Paul. Paul replicated Christ. Paul later entrusted this model to Timothy: "And what you have heard *from me* in the presence of many witnesses *entrust* to faithful men, who will be able to *teach others* also" (2 Tim 2:2). This encapsulates the aim of relational discipleship. We should live so that those who follow us end up near Christ. Relational discipleship replicates Christ's life in us.

WE NEED GOD'S POWER (VV. 18–21)

Even with Paul's corrective, relational approach, some in Corinth were unimpressed by Paul. They wrongly assumed this was a verbal warning, saying, "His letters are weighty and forceful, but in person he is unimpressive and his speaking amounts to nothing" (2 Cor 10:10). However, if they did not respond to Timothy, Paul was coming. He was coming as a loving father to discipline the disobedient Corinthians corporately. It is important to note that love without discipline is not love (Heb 12:6). If Christ's followers do not experience discipline, it fosters sinfulness. Conversely, discipline without love produces authoritarianism that drives people away from God.[7] The Corinthians did not need more debating, conversing, and talking. They needed the genuine power of God's kingdom.

God's kingdom is not demonstrated by speech alone but by *power* (δύναμις). Paul knew God's power would validate his talk—the edifying manifestations of the Holy Spirit, seeing lives transformed and humility lived out. Paul's message of power starkly contrasted the braggadocio and prideful focus of the Corinthians'

---

6. Soards, *1 Corinthians*, 103.
7. Blomberg, *1 Corinthians*, 96–97.

speech and knowledge. They focused more on rhetoric than God's transformational power.[8]

Unlike the Corinthian church, the contemporary church is not as fascinated by speech and knowledge but rather by relevance, appearance, and cultural acceptance. The trade-off is the lessening of God's power in the church. Sadly, numerous Western churches would not know what to do if the electricity went out during a church service. The focus has shifted from God's presence to stage production. The focus has shifted from pastoral shepherding to congregational spectating. The focus has shifted from missional living to occasional attending. The focus has shifted from the gospel's power to self-help. The focus has shifted from supernatural solutions to natural accommodations. The focus has shifted from faithful exposition of the Scriptures to communicative creativity. Church leaders, now is the time to return to the power of God's kingdom. We need a revival of Jesus' commission in action: "Heal the sick, raise the dead, cleanse lepers, cast out demons. You received without paying; give without pay" (Matt 10:8). We need the power of God's kingdom flowing in us and our churches.

KEY TAKEAWAYS

- Correction is a vital part of church life. When church leaders offer correction in the right spirit, it is an act of love rather than condemnation.

- Church leaders are not just information dispensers. God has called them to impart their life to those they lead. Their disciples will learn by proximity to their life's example.

- Church leaders must prioritize God's power over personal eloquence. God's kingdom is not about your words or knowledge but your ability to facilitate God's power among the people you lead.

---

8. Blomberg, *1 Corinthians*, 92.

REFLECT

1. How do you personally respond to correction? What steps can you take to grow in receiving it with humility?
2. How can you begin to model your life in a way that encourages others to imitate Christ through you?
3. Are there areas in your faith or ministry where you've focused more on appearances, eloquence, or relevance rather than God's power? How can you shift this focus?

CHAPTER SEVEN

Leaven in the Lump
Addressing Sin's Impact on the Church

> *Your boasting is not good. Do you not know that a little leaven leavens the whole lump? Cleanse out the old leaven that you may be a new lump, as you really are unleavened. For Christ, our Passover lamb, has been sacrificed. Let us therefore celebrate the festival, not with the old leaven, the leaven of malice and evil, but with the unleavened bread of sincerity and truth. I wrote to you in my letter not to associate with sexually immoral people—not at all meaning the sexually immoral of this world, or the greedy and swindlers, or idolaters, since then you would need to go out of the world. But now I am writing to you not to associate with anyone who bears the name of brother if he is guilty of sexual immorality or greed, or is an idolater, reviler, drunkard, or swindler—not even to eat with such a one. For what have I to do with judging outsiders? Is it not those inside the church whom you are to judge? God judges those outside. "Purge the evil person from among you."*
>
> — 1 Cor 5:6–13

INTRODUCTION

After discussing the possibility of coming with a corrective rod versus coming with love and a gentle Spirit, Paul described the Corinthian situations that warranted disciplinary action. A man in the Corinthian church was having relations with his father's wife. Jewish and Roman law prohibited this kind of behavior. Roman law required banishment to an island for this kind of offense.[1] Paul was shocked the Corinthians were proceeding as usual. He issued an immediate warning. The way Paul addressed this situation is a helpful guide for church leaders.

THE LIE OF A LITTLE (VV. 6-8)

In 1 Cor 5:2, Paul reprimanded the Corinthians because of their prideful toleration of sexual sin. One of their congregants was having relations with his father's wife.[2] Tolerating sexual sin is not something to be proud of. The resurrected, glorified Jesus told the church in Thyatira, "But I have this against you, that you *tolerate* that woman Jezebel, who calls herself a prophetess and is teaching and seducing my servants to *practice sexual immorality*" (Rev 2:20). Although our world celebrates tolerating sin, Jesus holds it against us. Tolerating sin is not virtuous. Christ does not admire it. The Corinthian church leaders ignored sexual sin and assumed it was a localized incident. They probably thought, "It's just one or two people. What does that matter?" They assumed sexual sin was an individual issue. Paul corrected their individualistic assumptions. The church is comprised of individuals but is a collective. Blatant, willful sin has severe effects on the entire church. It is a body. When one member of the body is sick, it affects the whole body.

Paul warned that this sin actively threatened their ability to remain holy and unified. This supposed minor issue was the little leaven threatening to leaven the whole lump. In antiquity, yeast

---

1. Barry et al., *Faithlife Study Bible*, 1 Cor 5:1.
2. Verbrugge, "1 Corinthians," 302.

was a familiar image illustrating a small matter's potential to affect the entire situation.[3] Paul made clear that there is no "little" immorality. Just as the Old Testament tabernacle was kept holy for God, the New Testament tabernacle, the church, must be kept holy. For this reason, church leaders must guard the church's holiness. They should never celebrate, condone, or boast about unrepentant sin within their members. Sin should cause tears. We should never cheer for what God cries over. The sin of sexual immorality and pride infected the Corinthian church as yeast does to dough.[4]

Paul's recommendation was fascinating: "*Cleanse* out the old leaven that you may be a new lump, as you really are unleavened" (1 Cor 5:7). Put simply, rid sexual immorality and pride from among yourselves. Be what you already are. The Corinthians were already unleavened by God's grace. They needed to let God's divine decree of identity inform their behavior.[5] Since God had declared them holy, act holy. Since God had declared them redeemed, act redeemed. Since God had cleansed them, act cleansed. Paul challenged them to act how God saw them.

What was the rationale behind Paul's conclusion? "For Christ, our Passover lamb, has been sacrificed" (1 Cor 5:7). It was customary at Passover to cleanse the home of all yeast to ensure the festival bread was unleavened. Paul connected this allusion to personal holiness. Christ, the eternal Passover lamb, paid the price for their holiness and ours. To ignore and pacify sin diminishes Christ's death, burial, resurrection, ascension, and exaltation.[6] To honor this sacrifice, God calls us to live in our divinely decreed identity where our actions are commensurate with God's decree of holiness.[7]

---

3. Soards, *1 Corinthians*, 114.
4. Verbrugge, "1 Corinthians," 303.
5. Ciampa and Rosner, *Corinthians*, 214.
6. Gardner, *1 Corinthians*, 233–34.
7. Soards, *1 Corinthians*, 115.

GUILTY BY ASSOCIATION (VV. 9-11)

Paul instructed the Corinthians not to associate with those continuing in unrepentant sin. This list was not exhaustive but included believers who were sexually immoral, greedy, idolaters, slanderers, drunkards, or swindlers. Church leaders should never condone these behaviors. As the adage goes, we live in the world but are not of the world (John 17:16). We are born from above (John 3:7), and our citizenship is in heaven (Phil 3:20). As unpopular as this message is, we must model God's countercultural standards before the watching world. Our holy separation from the world creates opportunities to share the glories of Christ's transforming power.

Paul encouraged the Corinthians not to eat with those who claimed Christ but lived in these unrepentant sins. Why? It creates guilt by association. Today's church struggles with Paul's admonition because we do not grasp our identity as a covenantal community responsible for honoring our individual and collective covenant with God. The church has been overwhelmed with cultural mindsets of tolerance that view accountability as judgmental, authoritarian, and unloving. This question resounds: "Who are we to judge?"[8] We are God's holy church and governing body in the earth:

- 1 Cor 6:3—"Do you not know that we are to *judge angels*? *How much more, then, matters pertaining to this life!*"

- Heb 12:12-17—"Therefore *lift* your drooping hands and *strengthen* your weak knees, and *make straight paths* for your feet, so that what is lame may not be put out of joint but rather be healed. Strive for peace with everyone, and *for the holiness without which no one will see the Lord*. See to it that no one fails to obtain the grace of God; that no 'root of bitterness' springs up and causes trouble, and by it many become defiled; that *no one is sexually immoral or unholy* like Esau, who sold his birthright for a single meal. For you know that afterward, when he desired to inherit the blessing, he was

---

8. Gardner, *1 Corinthians*, 242-43.

rejected, for he found no chance to repent, though he sought it with tears."

- Eph 5:27—"So that he might present the church to himself *in splendor, without spot or wrinkle or any such thing*, that she might be *holy and without blemish*."

Associating with people who live in unrepentant sin brings reproach to the church and Christ's name. Failing to address unrepentant sexual immorality exposed the Corinthian church to unnecessary criticism. Darkness remains where we refuse to shine God's exposing light. Rather than pacify and placate sin, may we lovingly and graciously call straying brothers and sisters back to the narrow path that leads to life (Matt 7:14).[9] The world's behaviors must never be the church's behavior.[10]

EXERCISING CHURCH DISCIPLINE (VV. 12-13)

Paul clarified that the church's role is not the judgment of the outside world. God judges them. Paul offered this prescription for engaging outsiders:

> If possible, so far as it depends on you, live peaceably with all. . . . "If your enemy is hungry, feed him; if he is thirsty, give him something to drink; for by so doing you will heap burning coals on his head." Do not be overcome by evil, but overcome evil with good. (Rom 12:18, 20–21)

Those outside belong to God's judgment. We show God's kindness, speak the truth in love, live righteously before them, and proclaim the good news of God's kingdom. The church is called to exercise discipline upon unrepentant sin for those inside.

Paul quoted Deut 17:7: "So you shall purge the evil from your midst." In context, Deut 17:7 refers to stoning Israelite idolaters. The Old Testament method of communal expulsion was death. In the New Testament, communal expulsion was spiritual and

---

9. Soards, *1 Corinthians*, 116.
10. Gardner, *1 Corinthians*, 238.

relational. A believer who commits egregious and unrepentant sins is no longer welcome to enjoy the church's fellowship. The church must return them to the world, hoping they will repent and return to God and His church. Drs. Ciampa and Rosner argue four reasons this man was expelled from the Corinthian church: "1. Being guilty of covenant disloyalty.... 2. The church is implicated in his sin.... 3. The community is the temple of the Holy Spirit.... 4. He must be ejected for his own sake."[11] Expulsion is not to harm the individual but to see their ultimate salvation and restoration. Living in unrepentant sin sets them up for eternal judgment. Church leaders who truly love their people will protect them, even if that means removing an unrepentant believer from fellowship for their ultimate good. The hope is that church discipline produces godly sorrow, which leads to true repentance.

When repentance happens, the individual can be fully restored to the church. Paul came to this conclusion in 2 Cor 2:5–11 about the man expelled from the Corinthian church:

> Now if anyone has caused pain, he has caused it not to me, but in some measure—not to put it too severely—to all of you. For such a one, this punishment by the majority is enough, so you should rather turn to forgive and comfort him, or he may be overwhelmed by excessive sorrow. So I beg you to reaffirm your love for him. For this is why I wrote, that I might test you and know whether you are obedient in everything. Anyone whom you forgive, I also forgive. Indeed, what I have forgiven, if I have forgiven anything, has been for your sake in the presence of Christ, so that we would not be outwitted by Satan; for we are not ignorant of his designs.

The aim of church discipline is healing, forgiveness, and reinstatement. May we be leaders committed to holiness, no matter the cost, carrying the ministry of healing and reconciliation.

---

11. Ciampa and Rosner, *Corinthians*, 220.

KEY TAKEAWAYS

- Just as a bit of leaven affects the entire lump of dough, sin contaminates the whole church community. Church leaders must take sin seriously, even when it seems minor.
- Church leaders should not adopt the world's sinful practices to reach the world. God calls us to His standard of holiness.
- While God is responsible for addressing sin outside the church, church leaders are responsible for addressing unrepentant sin within the church. Church discipline is always for the good of the unrepentant individual and the entire church body.

REFLECT

1. How can believers align their actions with their God-given identity of being holy?
2. How does tolerating sin among believers impact the church's witness to the world?
3. How can church leaders exercise discipline in a way that reflects both God's justice and His grace?

CHAPTER EIGHT

Presenting Your Body to God
A Temple for the Lord

"All things are lawful for me," but not all things are helpful. "All things are lawful for me," but I will not be dominated by anything. "Food is meant for the stomach and the stomach for food"—and God will destroy both one and the other. The body is not meant for sexual immorality, but for the Lord, and the Lord for the body. And God raised the Lord and will also raise us up by his power. Do you not know that your bodies are members of Christ? Shall I then take the members of Christ and make them members of a prostitute? Never! Or do you not know that he who is joined to a prostitute becomes one body with her? For, as it is written, "The two will become one flesh." But he who is joined to the Lord becomes one spirit with him. Flee from sexual immorality. Every other sin a person commits is outside the body, but the sexually immoral person sins against his own body. Or do you not know that your body is a temple of the Holy Spirit within you, whom you have from God? You are not your own, for you were bought with a price. So glorify God in your body.

— 1 Cor 6:12–20

INTRODUCTION

Paul rebuked a man within the Corinthian church for heinous sexual sin. It led to the nuclear option of church discipline—expulsion from the Corinthian church. With this issue in mind, Paul offered a theological rationale for why the Corinthians should be holy individually and collectively. He emphasized their collective, covenantal identity. They were not random individuals serving Christ. They were Christ's body. This passage helps church leaders understand the importance of holiness and purity for themselves and their churches.

MY BODY IS FOR THE LORD (VV. 12-14)

Paul rebuked the Corinthians with their maxim—"All things are lawful for me." This saying was derived from Gnostic thought, or the belief that the spirit and body were disconnected. The Corinthians concluded what they did physically did not impact them spiritually, giving them the false security that they were free to do whatever they physically desired.[1] Paul responded, "But not all things are helpful" (1 Cor 6:12). Even if an action does not violate a specific command, it does not mean it is helpful. The Greek term, *helpful* (συμφέρω), means it does not benefit someone else. It does not edify others. This reveals that freedoms should not be exercised because they can be. They should be exercised for the good of others. As a church leader, just because you can do something does not mean you should. Some leaders fight more for their freedoms in Christ than Christ Himself. They assume they can say, watch, and do whatever they please because "all things are lawful for me." They declare they are not under the law but under grace. The fundamental issue with this line of thinking is that the primary outcome of "freedom" is personal pleasure and self-gratification. The freedoms they fight for are rarely about the edification of others but the fulfillment of individual desires. Ascribing Christ's death

---

1. Trail, *Exegetical Summary*, 236.

for the rationale of self-gratifying, nonessential freedoms is an utter distortion of His sacrifice.

Paul quoted the Corinthians again—"All things are lawful for me." He responded, "But I will not be dominated by anything" (1 Cor 6:12). He cautioned that their dabbling in so-called freedoms caused enslavement to these so-called freedoms.[2] Dr. Barclay brilliantly said,

> The great fact of the Christian faith is not that it makes a man free to sin, but that it makes a man free *not* to sin.[3]

Dr. Prior adds,

> The man who has to express his freedom is actually in bondage to the need to show he is a free man. The genuinely free man has nothing to prove.[4]

I cannot tell you how many friends, ministry colleagues, and people argue with me about their so-called freedoms. I know one worship leader who was convinced Christ died for his freedom to smoke weed. He liked the feeling it gave him. I explained he was going to the wrong source. Peace was not in weed but in Christ. He was scared he would miss out on the freedom he felt if he quit smoking weed. I told him he was looking at the situation the wrong way. He was concerned about what he would lose if he quit weed. I was worried about what he would lose if he kept weed for peace, comfort, and fun. Anything you choose over Christ is an idol. It is not freedom. It is a fetter. One of my mentors once said, "The higher you want to go in God, the less freedoms you have."

In verse 13, Paul further cements this reality by quoting the Corinthians again: "Food is meant for the stomach and the stomach for food." The Corinthians used food as an argument to do whatever they wanted. Paul used this tangential argument about food to describe the deeper issue of sexual immorality. Food was a smokescreen to justify sexual immorality. Since the Corinthians

---

2. Verbrugge, "1 Corinthians," 310–11.
3. Barclay, *Letters*, 56–57; emphasis original.
4. Prior, *Message of 1 Corinthians*, 96.

argued that sexual relations were physical, their spirits would not be affected. How did Paul respond? "The body is meant for the Lord" (1 Cor 6:13). The body was uniquely created in God's image and will be raised on the last day. The body carries out the actions of our spirit. Dr. N. T. Wright says,

> In the present time the "body" is the locus and means of obedience, and as such is to be "presented" to God the creator for his service.[5]

God created the body for His purposes. It is an instrument for Him, not a means to fulfill our lusts and desires. Paul beautifully summarized this to the Romans: "Do not present your members to sin as *instruments for unrighteousness*, but present yourselves to God as those who have been brought from death to life, and your members to God as *instruments for righteousness*" (Rom 6:13).

MY BODY IS A MEMBER OF CHRIST (VV. 15–18)

In response, Paul asked a pointed question: "Do you not know that your bodies are members of Christ? . . . Or do you not know that he who is joined to a prostitute becomes one body with her?" (1 Cor 6:15–16). The Corinthians were infatuated with carnal, individualistic desires. What was Paul's response? "Your bodies are members of Christ" (v. 15). If they had relations with a prostitute, that individual joined him- or herself to the prostitute and, therefore, joined the entire body to the prostitute.[6] Paul clarified that what you do with your body impacts Christ's body.

Do not believe the ancient Gnostic lie that sexual relations are just physical. They are spiritual, and "they . . . become one flesh" (Gen 2:24). Any sexual act unites you with the other person. Your souls are knit together. Therefore, when a believer unites with a prostitute, Paul explained that Christ's body is united with that prostitute. This is what collective covenantal identity looks like. Unholy unions outside of holy matrimony betray our union

---

5. Wright, *Paul and the Faithfulness of God*, 491.
6. Barry et al., *Faithlife Study Bible*, 1 Cor 6:15.

with Christ and the collective body of Christ.[7] Here is a glorious mystery Paul revealed—"But he who is joined to the Lord becomes one spirit with him" (1 Cor 6:17). The way two people are joined through sexual intimacy parallels our spiritual union with God. Paul described it way in Eph 5:31–32: "'Therefore a man shall leave his father and mother and hold fast to his wife, and the two shall become one flesh.' This mystery is profound, and I am saying that it refers to Christ and the church." Our union with Christ is even closer than the sexual union between a husband and wife.[8] In this way, we are married to Christ. Therefore, any act that defiles this union is like defiling a marriage with a prostitute. My body is wholly committed to the Lord "as a living sacrifice, holy and acceptable to God" (Rom 12:1–2). We are united. Christ is in us, and we are in Christ.

Because of this spiritual reality, Paul commanded the Corinthians to *flee* (φεύγω) sexual immorality. The term *flee* (φεύγω) means to dash to escape it.[9] Unfortunately, we often placate sexual sin. We snuggle up to it. We test it. Instead, God calls us to flee from it. Joseph's example of running from Potiphar's wife illustrates this principle well. If you feel tempted, get up and run. Put your phone down and run. Get off the couch and run. Turn off the TV and run. Why? Sexual sin does not come from outside to defile within. It is different from something like drunkenness, where you drink a substance that affects your actions. Sexual immorality begins within and then defiles the body. Its impact is more detrimental than other sins.[10] If you do not believe me, ask David. He sinned in different ways in his life, but sexual sin caused the most significant damage. He and his children paid for it for the rest of his life. Sexual sin is not just against you. It is against Christ and His body. You actively harm yourself and expose yourself to an unholy union. As church leaders, we must remember that sexual sin is a sin against the people we commit to serve.

7. Verbrugge, "1 Corinthians," 312.
8. Ciampa and Rosner, *Corinthians*, 260.
9. Swanson, s.v. "φεύγω," *Dictionary of Biblical Languages*, §5771.
10. Ciampa and Rosner, *Corinthians*, 263.

MY BODY IS THE TEMPLE OF THE HOLY SPIRIT (VV. 19-20)

Paul returned to direct questioning, which is what good leaders do. They do not ramble in ambiguity but offer straightforward questions. "Do you not know . . . the Holy Spirit [lives inside] you?" (1 Cor 6:19). He urged them not to believe the Gnostic lie that their body was disconnected from their spirit. Their body, and ours, housed God's Holy Spirit. God will not just raise your body when the dead in Christ rise. He dwells in your body while you are alive. The Lord values your body so much that He lives in it.[11] When we think back to Old Testament stories, burning bushes that were not consumed enamor us (Exod 3). The pillar of fire enamors us (Exod 13). The Red Sea parting enamors us (Exod 14). The cloud that filled the tent of meeting enamors us (Exod 40). These should cause us to stand in awe of God. However, how does the fact that God lives in our mortal bodies not enamor us (Eph 3:17, Col 1:27)?

Since this is the case, we do not have sole autonomy over our bodies. What do I mean? We cannot do whatever we want because we "are not [our] own, for [we] were bought with a price" (1 Cor 6:19–20). This indicates two things:

1. *We were formerly owned by someone or something else.* We have a master, whether in sports, academia, lust, family, or money. Someone or something owns us. That is why Paul said a few verses prior, "And such were some of you. But you were washed, you were sanctified, you were justified in the name of the Lord Jesus Christ and by the Spirit of our God" (1 Cor 6:11).

2. *We were bought at a costly price.* We have new ownership. Jesus' costly blood purchased us. Peter said it this way: "Knowing that you were ransomed from the futile ways inherited from your forefathers, not with perishable things such as silver or gold, but with the precious blood of Christ" (1 Pet 1:18–19).

---

11. Verbrugge, "1 Corinthians," 312–13.

If you question your worth, know that you are worth Jesus' blood. Since He has purchased you by His blood, Paul argued we must glorify God with our bodies. After all, they are the Holy Spirit's temple.

Our physical body is a sacred gift we get to give to the Lord. As church leaders, may we faithfully offer our bodies to God in a holy and acceptable manner (Rom 12:1–2).

KEY TAKEAWAYS

- Personal freedoms should never be a church leader's primary focus. The church's edification and witness are more important than self-gratifying "freedoms."
- Church leaders must remain holy before the Lord and dedicated to His purposes. We are not our own. The way we live impacts everyone around us.
- Sexual sin is not only a personal sin against your own body but a collective sin against Christ's body. Church leaders must set an example by fleeing from sexual sin rather than indulging in it.

REFLECT

1. How does Paul's emphasis on the church's collective, covenantal identity challenge your view of personal holiness?
2. What freedoms in your life may not be helpful or edifying to others?
3. How can you glorify God with your body practically as a church leader?

CHAPTER NINE

Sacrificial Leadership
A Foundation of Love

Now concerning food offered to idols: we know that "all of us possess knowledge." This "knowledge" puffs up, but love builds up. If anyone imagines that he knows something, he does not yet know as he ought to know. But if anyone loves God, he is known by God. Therefore, as to the eating of food offered to idols, we know that "an idol has no real existence," and that "there is no God but one." For although there may be so-called gods in heaven or on earth—as indeed there are many "gods" and many "lords"—yet for us there is one God, the Father, from whom are all things and for whom we exist, and one Lord, Jesus Christ, through whom are all things and through whom we exist. However, not all possess this knowledge. But some, through former association with idols, eat food as really offered to an idol, and their conscience, being weak, is defiled. Food will not commend us to God. We are no worse off if we do not eat, and no better off if we do. But take care that this right of yours does not somehow become a stumbling block to the weak. For if anyone sees you who have knowledge eating in an idol's temple, will he not be encouraged, if his conscience is weak, to eat food offered to idols? And so by your knowledge this weak person is destroyed, the brother for whom Christ died. Thus, sinning against your brothers and wounding their conscience when it is weak, you sin against Christ. Therefore, if food makes my brother stumble, I will never eat meat, lest I make my brother stumble.

— 1 COR 8:1-13

INTRODUCTION

In this passage, Paul addressed the common practice of eating food sacrificed to idols. Although this may seem foreign, this custom was intricately woven into ancient eating practices. Archaeological discoveries reveal ancient pagan temples functioned as restaurants as well.[1] This is textually evidenced by Paul stating that some ate in idolatrous temples. Against this backdrop, Paul addressed a broader principal imperative for church leaders in an hour of unholy mixture, societal demise, and cultural collapse—sacrificial love.

THE FOUNDATION OF TRUE KNOWLEDGE (VV. 1-3)

The early church wanted to distance itself from the idol worship cult. The first church council in Jerusalem determined three practices to avoid the influence of gentile idol worship: (1) avoid food sacrificed to idols, (2) blood from strangled animals, and (3) sexual immorality (Acts 15:29).[2] Such regulation would prevent gentiles from going back to false worship. The Corinthians faced a conundrum. Most of the meat in Corinth was leftovers from pagan temple sacrifices.[3] This created issues for those saved from pagan

---

1. Keown, *Gospels and Acts*, 72.
2. Gardner, *1 Corinthians*, 366.
3. Blomberg, *1 Corinthians*, 159.

religious practices. What were Corinthian Christians supposed to do in a society filled with this marketplace practice?

As Paul did before, he quoted a common saying among the Corinthians: "All of us possess knowledge" (1 Cor 8:1). They bragged that they possessed the grace-gift of knowledge and were beyond being bothered by food sacrificed to idols.[4] They knew that idols were meaningless because there was only one God and felt they could feast on the food sacrificed to idols without issue. Paul found a significant problem with their so-called knowledge. Why? Their knowledge made them proud. The term *puffs up* (φυσιόω) literally means they were inflated with air. Their knowledge made them arrogant, prideful, and airheaded as they flaunted a grace-gift.[5] They thought their knowledge evidenced spiritual depth. Ironically, their knowledge without love meant they lacked actual knowledge.[6] Knowledge from God is woven in love that builds people up. It constructs and edifies other believers. It does not put them in potentially compromising positions for so-called freedoms.

I'll never forget when my wife and I led fifty people to an all-day prayer event on the National Mall. On the ride, the bus driver decided to put on a movie. The movie was a PG-13 movie but opened with foul language and violence. I felt the Holy Spirit being grieved. We were on the way to a prayer event, simultaneously soiling our souls with ungodly content. I kindly asked the bus driver to turn off the movie. He did. I then announced to the bus that I decided to turn the film off because it was not spiritually edifying or preparing us for the event we were headed to. There were a few sighs of frustration. No one said anything. I sat back down, knowing I had done the right thing, but I felt the silence behind me. As people exited the bus, one elderly lady thanked me for turning the movie off. She explained that knowing and doing the right thing is different. Spiritual knowledge benefits and builds up other believers toward righteousness, holiness, and purity. It does not lead them to compromise. Actual spiritual knowledge is not

---

4. Barry et al., *Faithlife Study Bible*, 1 Cor 8:1.
5. Verbrugge, "1 Corinthians," 330.
6. Barry et al., *Faithlife Study Bible*, 1 Cor 8:2.

data collection. If knowledge does not inform godly behavior, it is not true knowledge. It is useless. It will cause you to be airheaded. God's knowledge and love for us are the foundation and revelation of true knowledge.

THE THEOLOGICAL WHY (VV. 4-7)

To steer the conversation further, Paul again quoted their conclusions that "an idol has no real existence" and that "there is no God but one" (v. 4). The Corinthians were right, in part. They were right that an idol is an inanimate object with no power to save, deliver, or rescue. However, their conclusion led to their justification of eating food sacrificed to idols.[7] They did not grasp that idols create space for demonic, malevolent spirits to flourish. They were right in the monotheistic conclusion that "there is no God but one." They were wrong in not accounting for demonic spirits. Even though idols are not gods, they are portals for demonic activity. That is why Paul said, "No, I imply that what pagans sacrifice they offer to demons and not to God. I do not want you to be participants with demons. You cannot drink the cup of the Lord and the cup of demons. You cannot partake of the table of the Lord and the table of demons" (1 Cor 10:20-21).

Paul did not tolerate idol worship and the pursuit of so-called gods. As a Pharisee, Paul knew the Hebrews' expansive history with idols, ultimately leading them into exile. After returning from Babylonian exile in 536 BC, the Jewish people wanted to remove themselves from idol worship, sparking religious fervor against it. Therefore, Paul was deeply angered when he saw the streets of Athens lined with idols (Acts 17:16), while praising the Thessalonians for "turning to God from idols to serve the living and true God" (1 Thess 1:9). That is why he urged the Corinthians to "flee from idolatry" (1 Cor 10:7). The Corinthians' so-called knowledge threatened to lead people into demonic worship.[8] Church leaders

---

7. Barry et al., *Faithlife Study Bible*, 1 Cor 8:4.
8. Verbrugge, "1 Corinthians," 331.

should never champion knowledge that may lead people into sin. Paul certainly did not. When church leaders are desensitized to the spiritual threats surrounding them, they cannot sound the alarm. The Levitical principle stands: priests "shall be holy to their God and not profane the name of their God. For they offer the LORD's food offerings, the bread of their God; therefore they shall be holy" (Lev 21:6). When church leaders live holy to God, they can see the unholiness that threatens them and their people.

To further develop the Corinthians' understanding of monotheism, Paul included Jesus in his reconfiguration of the Jewish Shema from Deut 6:4: "Hear, O Israel: The Lord our God, the Lord is one."[9] Who is the Lord? Jesus is Lord: "Yet for us there is one God, the Father, from whom are all things and for whom we exist, and *one Lord, Jesus Christ*, through whom are all things and through whom we exist" (1 Cor 8:6). "All things exist through Him" (Col 1:16), and "in him we live and move and have our being" (Acts 17:28). These so-called pagan gods cannot create. They cannot bring anything into existence. They cannot bring you from death to life. They are lifeless shells full of deceptive demonic entities. Paul needed the Corinthians to grasp this foundational reality in a region pilfered with idolatry. He described it this way to the church at Colossae:

> He is the image of the invisible God, the firstborn of all creation. For by him all things were created, in heaven and on earth, visible and invisible, whether thrones or dominions or rulers or authorities—all things were created through him and for him. And he is before all things, and in him all things hold together. And he is the head of the body, the church. He is the beginning, the firstborn from the dead, that in everything he might be preeminent. For in him all the fullness of God was pleased to dwell, and through him to reconcile to himself all things, whether on earth or in heaven, making peace by the blood of his cross. (Col 1:15–20)

---

9. Barry et al., *Faithlife Study Bible*, 1 Cor 8:4.

The problem the Corinthians faced was not in the reality of false idols. It was this: those delivered from demonic worship were being lured back in by prideful Corinthians who said it did not matter because the idols were not real. Paul warned them "not all possess this knowledge. But some, through former association with idols, eat food as really offered to an idol, and their conscience, being weak, is defiled" (1 Cor 8:7). In the name of so-called knowledge, Corinthian leaders brought back past demonic religious experiences for recent converts who did not have theological and spiritual foundations to handle nuanced freedom. Church leaders must understand the theological *why* before they present a carte blanche slate of so-called freedoms any believer can indulge in. Paul offered a helpful paradigm for how to respond in the following verses.

THE RIGHT RESPONSE (VV. 8–13)

Paul again quoted the Corinthians: "Food will not commend us to God. We are no worse off if we do not eat, and no better off if we do" (v. 8). Paul did not argue that food is good or bad. He agreed that it is neutral. Its intent is nourishment. However, Paul warned the Corinthians not to allow eating to become a stumbling block for the weak.

Here was the issue. The Corinthians not only ate food sacrificed to idols. They ate food sacrificed to idols in pagan temples—the restaurants of antiquity. It would be like this: You were a person with alcoholism, and God radically delivered you from crippling alcoholism. The week after being freed from alcoholism, your Christian friend invites you over for a beer. They claim they are free to enjoy alcohol. However, their so-called knowledge about freedoms endangers the recently freed alcoholic. This was Corinth's situation with recent converts from idol worship. When they lived their so-called liberties, they were sending weaker believers back into the hands of idols.

Paul strategically reapplied the term *encouraged* (οἰκοδομέω), which he previously used to describe how love builds up fellow believers. Rather than building converts in the love of God,

Corinthian leaders *built up* (οἰκοδομέω) converts to worship idols. The Corinthian leaders' so-called knowledge and so-called freedoms destroyed converts who Christ died for. Paul used the term *destroy* (ἀπόλλυμι) which most commonly refers to someone eternally lost. These new Corinthian converts were being led from life back to death, freedom back to bondage, and light back to darkness because of so-called freedoms. May we never cause people to revert from where God has delivered them. Church leaders must seek to build up their people in love rather than placate their own pleasures, thereby destroying those God entrusts to them.

Paul warned this was not just a sin against the convert but against Christ Himself. Paul knew the pain of sinning against Christ. That was Paul's revelatory introduction to Jesus on the Damascus road—"I am Jesus, whom you are *persecuting*" (Acts 9:5). When you sin against those who have Christ in them, you sin against Christ Himself. Christ did not die to advance personal pleasures that come at the expense of Christian brothers and sisters. If you choose that path, you are directly offending and sinning against Christ.

Love inspired Paul to give up meat for the rest of his life if need be. Paul's sacrificial stance is instructive for church leaders. We must take precautions to ensure our brothers and sisters do not stumble. We demonstrate love through sacrifice. Christ modeled this perfectly on the cross: "Greater love has no one than this, that someone lay down his life for his friends" (John 15:13). True knowledge grasps the law of love that motivates biblical, sacrificial action. Church leaders should not be guided by what they can do that is permissible. Instead, we must take a posture like this: To what lengths am I willing to inconvenience myself for the salvation and growth of those God has entrusted to me? For the sake of others, may we operate with love, the foundation of true knowledge.

KEY TAKEAWAYS

- Knowledge without love causes harmful hubris. Church leaders should prioritize true spiritual knowledge and its rootedness in love rather than proving how much they know.
- Church leaders must address the demonic forces that lure people into bondage and oppression.
- Church leaders must be willing to sacrifice their freedoms for the sake of others. They never want to harm those God has entrusted them to lead.

REFLECT

1. Are there areas where you prioritize knowledge over love in your life with God?
2. How does understanding the spiritual reality behind idols (e.g., demonic activity) change your perspective on seemingly neutral practices?
3. How does Paul's willingness to sacrifice his freedom for the sake of others challenge your approach to Christian leadership or discipleship?

CHAPTER TEN

The Key to Effective Ministry
Serving with Discipline and Purpose

For though I am free from all, I have made myself a servant to all, that I might win more of them. To the Jews I became as a Jew, in order to win Jews. To those under the law I became as one under the law (though not being myself under the law) that I might win those under the law. To those outside the law I became as one outside the law (not being outside the law of God but under the law of Christ) that I might win those outside the law. To the weak I became weak, that I might win the weak. I have become all things to all people, that by all means I might save some. I do it all for the sake of the gospel, that I may share with them in its blessings. Do you not know that in a race all the runners run, but only one receives the prize? So run that you may obtain it. Every athlete exercises self-control in all things. They do it to receive a perishable wreath, but we an imperishable. So I do not run aimlessly; I do not box as one beating the air. But I discipline my body and keep it under control, lest after preaching to others I myself should be disqualified.

— 1 Cor 9:19–27

THE KEY TO EFFECTIVE MINISTRY

INTRODUCTION

We explored the importance of limiting freedoms for the sake of others. The apostle Paul's nuanced approach balances this truth as he considered the Corinthians' personal, cultural, and relational needs while serving them.[1] Ministry does not happen in a vacuum but within the context a person is ministering. However, this passage does not justify unholy ministerial approaches. Its misinterpretation and subsequent misappropriation have been detrimental to many churches.

SERVING TO SEE SALVATION (VV. 19-23)

Paul never wanted cultural differences to be a stumbling block to salvation.[2] The gospel does not belong to any specific culture. It takes root within culture, transforming the culture into the kingdom's culture. There is, however, nuance in every cultural expression.[3] If you attend a Brazilian church, it may feel familiar but different. If you attend an Asian church, it may feel familiar but different. If you attend a European church, it may feel familiar but different. If you attend an African church, it may feel familiar but different. Paul was free from all obligations within various cultures. Nonetheless, he made himself a servant for the sake of their salvation.

This does not mean Paul violated Scripture to reach people. Paul was not a chameleon that appeased every group. He never changed his message. He was clear to the Galatian church, "If any man preaches another gospel, let him be accursed" (Gal 1:8-9). He publicly rebuked Peter for acting one way with Jewish people and another way with gentiles (Gal 2:11-21). Contemporary church leaders have distorted this text to validate ministry approaches full of compromise in the name of reaching people. Contextualization of the gospel does not mean compromise. The message never

---

1. Verbrugge, "1 Corinthians," 338.
2. Gardner, *1 Corinthians*, 404.
3. Ciampa and Rosner, *Corinthians*, 425.

changes. However, we must know how to present the message in various contexts. Dr. Carson summarizes this beautifully:

> The message of the Lord Christ, crucified and raised, who demands love and the obedience of faith, must not be changed (Gal 1:9–11). Many will turn away from this message, and many who appear to believe will eventually walk away (Luke 8:9–15; 2 Cor 4:3), but Paul is content to leave that in God's hands (1 Thess 1:4–5). However, he is prepared to sacrifice his personal social and cultural preferences if they might cloud the message of Christ.[4]

Paul did not unnecessarily offend people or put barriers between the people and the gospel message.[5] Therefore, *to the Jews*, he became like a Jew. To *those under the law*, he became as under the law. The irony is Paul was a Jew. He lived blamelessly under the law according to Phil 3:6. However, since he experienced salvation by grace, his Pharisaical approach changed (Eph 2:8–10). When Paul ministered to his Jewish brothers and sisters, he did not disparage their fidelity to the law as he tried to reach them—for example, Timothy, who accompanied Paul on his second missionary journey. Paul made Timothy get circumcised. Why? An uncircumcised Jew in the synagogue created unnecessary barriers to Jewish people receiving the gospel message (Acts 16:2). Good church leaders are willing to inconvenience themselves to limit unnecessary offense.

To *those not under the law*, Paul did not demand they celebrate Jewish festivals. He did not require they be circumcised. He did not demand they go to a rabbinical school. He proclaimed the gospel message and lived by the law of Christ—Christ's teachings and the way of sacrificial love (Mark 10:45). Paul did not impose Jewish law on those not under the law.

To the weak, Paul became weak. The weak were those recent converts teetering from the pull of former idolatrous practices. Paul did not flaunt freedoms but abstained from meat sacrificed to idols. He rejected any action that would unnecessarily create a stumbling block to their receptivity and growth in the gospel.

4. Carson, *Becoming Conversant*, 120.
5. Witherington, *Conflict and Community*, 211.

Paul became all things to all people to win as many as possible to Christ. Dr. Garland offers this summary of Paul's approach:

> He does not think that fundamental and distinctive demands are negotiable, depending on the circumstances. . . . He did not tone down his assault on idolatry to avoid offending idolaters or to curry favor with them. His accommodation has nothing to do with watering down the gospel message, soft-pedaling its ethical demands, or compromising its absolute monotheism. Paul never modified the message of Christ crucified to make it less of a scandal to Jews or less foolish to Greeks.[6]

Paul wanted to make a good impression on unbelieving people so they would not immediately reject the gospel message because of offense. Paul wanted to see the people to whom he preached experience salvation. Imagine ministering at a church that expected ministers to wear suits, but you decided to preach in jeans and a T-shirt. Nothing is particularly sinful about preaching in jeans and a T-shirt; however, you unnecessarily offend the hearers by dismissing their concerns. Offending people when you do not have to is unfruitful. Good church leaders serve to see people experience God's salvation and redemption.

RUN TO WIN (VV. 24–25)

Paul used an athletic metaphor to redirect their attention: "Do you not know that in a race all the runners run, but only one receives the prize?" (v. 24). This metaphor was significant for the Corinthians. Their city hosted the Isthmian Games, one of four primary Greek competitions which occurred every other year.[7] In antiquity, there were no team sports. Every athletic game was an individual competition.[8] Months before the event, athletes would engage in a

---

6. Garland, *1 Corinthians*, 435.
7. Ciampa and Rosner, *Corinthians*, 435–36.
8. Verbrugge, "1 Corinthians," 340.

restricted diet, self-denial, and constant training.[9] Paul leveraged this context for the Christian life. If athletes were willing to exercise such restraint for a crown of withering leaves, how much more should Christians train for life's race that results in an unfading, imperishable crown? How much more should Christians want that glorious crown to be cast at Jesus' feet?

Church leaders, we are not competing against each other for a singular prize. We live with the same tenacity as an athlete who trains to win a competition. We want to run life's race to receive Jesus' commendation at the finish line: "Well done, good and faithful servant. . . . Enter into the joy of your master" (Matt 25:23).

Do seriousness and discipline mark your life with God? Do you want to win the race? Are you just attempting to hobble across the finish line? Have you ever wondered why we are so apathetic in our spiritual life but give inordinate attention to sports, games, competitions, shows, and hobbies? Do not be blinded by the god of this world to the eternal glories of the unfading, imperishable crown. Paul warned the Corinthians, "In their case the god of this world has blinded the minds of the unbelievers, to keep them from seeing the light of the gospel of the glory of Christ, who is the image of God" (2 Cor 4:4). Prideful Corinthian Christians bragged about their spiritual superiority. Paul humbled them by reminding them that being an athlete does not guarantee a crown. None of us living have crossed the finish line yet. We must not get casual and relaxed. We must run to win with our eyes fixed on Jesus as we wait for Him to crown us with the crown of unfading glory (1 Pet 5:4).

DISCIPLINED TO WIN (VV. 26–27)

Paul tied everything together with two final metaphors. Paul did not run in a zigzag. He did not go back and forth. He did not waiver between two opinions. He did not run like he did not know where he was going. Paul had a straight line—Christ. Paul emphasized this point with his second metaphor: He did "not box as one

---

9. Trail, *Exegetical Summary*, 365.

beating the air" (v. 26). Put differently, Paul did not shadowbox without ever getting into the ring. When he boxed, he hit the mark. Many church leaders say they are running the race but are zigzagging around by focusing on metrics, social media, and human methodologies. While none of these things are bad in and of themselves, they leave church leaders shipwrecked when Christ is not the focus. Many church leaders say they are boxing but are hitting the air with performative preaching analyzed by group opinion. We need church leaders who fix their eyes on Jesus. We need alignment between what church leaders say and what they do.

Like an athlete, Paul disciplined his body to keep it under control. Just as an athlete has a diet and training plan, Paul had a spiritual plan. Paul diligently removed the areas in his life that opposed God's purposes in him. I recently heard a church leader say, "I should not have said that, but it felt good." Good church leaders restrain themselves, exercising discipline and wisdom. We must live in a disciplined way that subjects areas of weakness and temptation to God's Word and ways. Beyond restraining weaknesses, Paul also disciplined areas of personal freedom. By exercising certain freedoms, they would have limited his reach. His self-discipline extended beyond weaknesses to any area that would hinder him from being a more effective witness for Christ.[10] May we be disciplined to win others and receive that glorious, unfading, imperishable crown.

Paul did not want to preach to everyone else and be disqualified for neglecting God's Word and ways. I am reminded of countless Olympic relay runners. Many dropped the baton or passed the baton outside the takeoff zone. Both resulted in disqualification. They ran well but became disqualified. This sobering illustration reminds church leaders that no matter how well we run at any given time, we must stay disciplined for life's whole race. If not, we may be disqualified at the race's end.

---

10. Trail, *Exegetical Summary*, 369.

KEY TAKEAWAYS

- Attempts to reach the world should never compromise the cross's message.
- Church leaders must exercise discipline in every area of their life and ministry. Our goal is not human acknowledgment but the imperishable crown given by God.
- Church leaders must not become distracted by worldly pursuits. Distraction derails kingdom effectiveness.
- Church leaders must remain faithful throughout their *entire* life. Failing to maintain focus and discipline may result in their disqualification.

REFLECT

1. Reflect on Paul's balance between contextualizing the message and holding firm to biblical truths. How can you practice this balance in your ministry and personal witness?
2. Consider the things you invest your time, energy, and passion into. Are you pursuing an imperishable crown, or are you distracted by temporary, worldly goals?
3. Paul warned of the danger of being "disqualified" despite preaching to others. What safeguards can you implement to ensure your private life aligns with your public ministry?

CHAPTER ELEVEN

Supernatural Stewardship
Shepherding Spiritual Gifts with Wisdom

> *Now concerning spiritual gifts, brothers, I do not want you to be uninformed. You know that when you were pagans you were led astray to mute idols, however you were led. Therefore I want you to understand that no one speaking in the Spirit of God ever says "Jesus is accursed!" and no one can say "Jesus is Lord" except in the Holy Spirit. Now there are varieties of gifts, but the same Spirit; and there are varieties of service, but the same Lord; and there are varieties of activities, but it is the same God who empowers them all in everyone. To each is given the manifestation of the Spirit for the common good. For to one is given through the Spirit the utterance of wisdom, and to another the utterance of knowledge according to the same Spirit, to another faith by the same Spirit, to another gifts of healing by the one Spirit, to another the working of miracles, to another prophecy, to another the ability to distinguish between spirits, to another various kinds of tongues, to another the interpretation of tongues. All these are empowered by one and the same Spirit, who apportions to each one individually as he wills.*
>
> — 1 Cor 12:1–11

INTRODUCTION

Because of the Corinthians' pervasive misuse of spiritual gifts, the apostle Paul presented the purpose and functionality of spiritual gifts within the congregational setting. This topic was so important it warranted a chapters-long discussion.[1] Even though many church leaders have shifted away from spiritual gifts in the congregational setting, Paul offers helpful guidance for stewarding and shepherding God's gifts for the church's edification.

BEING TEACHABLE ABOUT SPIRITUAL GIFTS (VV. 1-2)

Although the Corinthians thought they had mastered spiritual gifts, Paul did "not want [them] to be uninformed" (v. 1). Paul urged the Corinthians to maintain a posture of humility since spiritual gifts are unmerited *grace-gifts* (χάρισμα) given by God. They are not acquired by secret knowledge. Therefore, the Corinthians needed to drop their egotistic attitude.[2] Why? None of us have room for boasting—spiritual gifts are God's gifts. Corinthian arrogance proved that they were not as knowledgeable as they thought. Unfortunately, the Corinthian mindset about spiritual gifts still exists. Some people still think they know everything about spiritual gifts without room to learn. There is no mystery.

The Corinthians' other error was believing their former pagan spiritual experience prepared them to understand and operate in spiritual gifts.[3] Dr. Verbrugge explains

> that some Corinthians at one time likely participated in pagan religious practices that involved influence from demons, ecstatic or mantic speech, practices that we now associate with the occult and the like. It is not impossible, therefore, that the debates in Corinth over speaking in

---

1. Verbrugge, "1 Corinthians," 362.
2. Witherington, *Conflict and Community*, 255.
3. Ciampa and Rosner, *Corinthians*, 562–63.

tongues ranged over whether and how this phenomenon was different from pagan ecstatic speech.[4]

Their previous spiritual experiences could not, however, be trusted as a guide for God's *grace-gifts* (χάρισμα).[5] Some people are still converted from dark, pagan backgrounds; however, most in the Western world come from spiritual skepticism. Enlightenment thinking has permeated the Western world, reducing everything to rational perception and limiting the reception of true knowledge and divine revelation by the Spirit.[6]

To remedy their lack of knowledge, Paul explained three essential truths to the Corinthians:

1. They were uninformed about spiritual gifts.
2. They filtered their understanding through pagan experiences.
3. They needed guidelines about spiritual things.[7]

These were the difficult truths the Corinthians needed to hear. Good church leaders share the truth with their people even when it is difficult.

Paul desperately wanted the Corinthians to be informed about spiritual gifts before they started wielding them. Church leaders are responsible for shepherding and teaching the members of the body how to identify and utilize their spiritual gifts. Spiritual gifts are powerful. They are mighty spiritual weapons (2 Cor 10:4). Before people wield them, they need training. False and inappropriate usages of spiritual gifts can deeply wound people. We must be informed to tell others how to use spiritual gifts healthily and in an orderly manner. This approach is much healthier than suppressing them out of fear or control.

---

4. Verbrugge, "1 Corinthians," 363.
5. Ciampa and Rosner, *Corinthians*, 562–63.
6. Ciampa and Rosner, *Corinthians*, 562–63.
7. Gardner, *1 Corinthians*, 528.

GOD GIVES VARIOUS GIFTS (VV. 4–10)

Spiritual gifts are not just the Holy Spirit's gifts. Paul taught the Corinthians that spiritual gifts were Trinitarian gifts: "The same Spirit; . . . the same Lord; . . . the same God" (vv. 4–6). The Father, Son, and Holy Spirit are delighted to give spiritual gifts for the church's edification. Let us explore how each member of the Trinity participates in distributing spiritual gifts.

1. *The Holy Spirit*—"There are varieties of gifts, but the same Spirit" (v. 4). *Varieties* (διαίρεσις) underscore the unique gifts made available. *Gifts* (χάρισμα) illustrate the Holy Spirit's gracious distribution of spiritual gifts. While spiritual gifts range from teaching to speaking in other languages, the Holy Spirit is the one behind them all.

2. *Jesus*—"There are varieties of service, but the same Lord" (v. 5). *Service* (διακονία) indicates these gifts should not be used for self-aggrandizement. They are used in service to God and others. They are not given to prove how spiritual we are. They are given to show how the Lord Jesus has equipped us to serve. He is the chief *servant* (διάκονος) of all. Spiritual gifts enable us to serve others better and model Jesus' servitude. Church leaders must help others view spiritual gifts as a service to Christ and His body. The body and the world desperately need the "varieties of services."

3. *God*—"There are varieties of activities, but it is the same God who empowers them all" (v. 6). *Activities* (ἐνέργημα) describes effective, miraculous power.[8] Put simply, God gives us the power to perform divine services for the body of Christ.[9] He is the active agent behind the powerful working of spiritual gifts.

Of these varieties, "each is given the manifestation of the Spirit for the common good" (v. 7). Although many in Christ's body believe

---

8. BDAG, s.v. "ἐνέργημα."
9. Trail, *Exegetical Summary*, 124.

they do not have spiritual gifts, the apostle Paul disagrees. You may not currently operate in or recognize spiritual gifts; however, "*each is given the manifestation of the Spirit for the common good.*" These are not gifts you are born with. They are supernatural gifts God gives. Therefore, no one in Christ's body can say God passed them by when He handed out spiritual gifts.[10]

Nine spiritual gifts further illustrate God's variety. This list of nine is only a partial list of God's gifts. Additional lists are found in Rom 12:3–8 and Eph 4:11. Some differentiate these lists as describing personal, ministry, ordinary, and supernatural gifts. Regardless of their description, they are God-given gifts.[11]

1. *The Utterance of Wisdom* describes the ability to speak with divine wisdom and insight beyond human rationality or understanding, enabling the application of truth to a situation.[12] The emphasis of this gift "is not on wisdom itself but on the word or message produced by that wisdom. . . . Biblical wisdom involves discerning what God would have someone do as a result of that observation (e.g., Prov 8:1, 20–21, 22–24; compare Jas 1:5)."[13] The utterance of wisdom is valuable and helpful in giving guidance in difficult situations where it seems like there is no way out. Jesus modeled the word of wisdom in John 8:7 when a woman was caught in adultery and brought to be stoned. Jesus drew in the sand and said, "Let him who is without sin among you be the first to throw a stone at her." Church leaders desperately need the ability to share information with those they lead beyond their rational capabilities.

2. *The Utterance of Knowledge* describes the ability to speak spiritual words of revelation.[14] This includes proclaiming deep truths about Scripture and understanding spiritual

---

10. Verbrugge, "1 Corinthians," 365.
11. Verbrugge, "1 Corinthians," 365.
12. Trail, *Exegetical Summary*, 128.
13. Barry et al., *Faithlife Study Bible*, 1 Cor 12:8.
14. Trail, *Exegetical Summary*, 129.

mysteries.[15] The utterance of knowledge may also describe knowing someone's life or situation without any previous knowledge. This is what I call *divine intelligence*. Put simply, God gives you information you could not obtain otherwise. This was evidenced in Jesus' life in John 4:18 when He told the woman at the well, "For you have had five husbands, and the one you now have is not your husband. What you have said is true." The utterance of knowledge powerfully communicates God's heart toward people. Church leaders need to communicate information beyond what they have learned.

3. *The Gift of Faith* differs from saving faith. It describes faith in God to accomplish the impossible. Jesus described this faith when His disciples asked Him why they could not drive out the demon from the twelve-year-old boy: "He replied, 'Because you have so little faith. Truly I tell you, if you have faith as small as a mustard seed, you can say to this mountain, "Move from here to there," and it will move. Nothing will be impossible for you'" (Matt 17:20). The gift of faith is the supernatural assurance God will accomplish the impossibility before you.[16] You know it will happen because God has given you the gift of faith. Church leaders need the gift of faith when we pray for breakthroughs in our personal life and ministry.

4. *The Gifts of Healing(s)* is plural, not singular. It describes the different gifts of healing for different kinds of ailments.[17] When we pray for healing, we need gifts of healing(s) for specific maladies, diseases, and ailments. Jesus healed all kinds of diseases and has commissioned us to do the same: "Heal the sick, raise the dead, cleanse lepers, cast out demons" (Matt 10:8). Church leaders need the gifts of healing(s) to see God's healing power flow through the body of Christ.

---

15. Blomberg, *1 Corinthians*, 244.
16. Trail, *Exegetical Summary*, 130.
17. Blomberg, *1 Corinthians*, 244.

5. *The Working of Miracles* is translated as "activities of power" that are supernatural and miraculous.[18] They describe supernatural activities like exorcising demons, raising the dead, and God's other unexpected, powerful acts.[19] We need the working of miracles flowing through our churches. We must join the prayer of the early church leaders: "While you stretch out your hand to heal, and signs and wonders are performed through the name of your holy servant Jesus" (Acts 4:30).

6. *Prophecy* is best understood as a Holy Spirit–inspired message with elements of forthtelling and foretelling for others' edification.[20] Forthtelling is the proclamation of God's words and thoughts on a matter. Foretelling is the announcement of future events before they occur. Although prophecy occurs in forthtelling and foretelling, it should never be tried on people. People are not test subjects. They are precious to God. Trying out prophecy on people is very damaging. When the gift of prophecy functions, the prophecy is correct. Why? God is speaking through the person prophesying. Church leaders can determine prophetic accuracy through these litmus tests:

    1. It aligns with Scripture.
    2. Two or more people confirm it.
    3. The Holy Spirit confirms it.

7. *The Distinguishing of Spirits* empowers someone to recognize the origin and purpose of an utterance, attitude, or atmosphere.[21] We desperately need the distinguishing of spirits to uncover root problems in our personal lives and ministerial service. The apostle Paul offers a powerful example of the distinguishing of spirits. In Acts 13:8–10, Elymas, the sorcerer, opposed Paul's ministry. Paul discerned and addressed the demonic spirit behind his opposition: "Then Saul, who was

---

18. Trail, *Exegetical Summary*, 131.
19. Gardner, *1 Corinthians*, 537.
20. Trail, *Exegetical Summary*, 132.
21. Barry et al., *Faithlife Study Bible*, 1 Cor 12:10.

also called Paul, filled with the Holy Spirit, looked straight at Elymas and said, 'You are a child of the devil and an enemy of everything that is right! You are full of all kinds of deceit and trickery. Will you never stop perverting the right ways of the Lord?'" If we do not know the origin of opposition, how can we adequately address it?

8. *Kinds of Tongues* describe foreign and spiritual languages.[22] It is the ability to speak unlearned human languages, angelic languages, or ecstatic spiritual utterances.[23] Paul thanked God that he "pray[ed] in tongues more than all of you" (1 Cor 14:18). He wanted the Corinthian church to have a proper understanding of the gift of tongues so that the body of Christ could be edified. Church leaders need to teach about and personally experience the gift of various kinds of tongues for personal and corporate edification.

9. *Interpretation of Tongues* is the ability to translate or interpret what is said through the gift of tongues.[24] This enables the body of believers to be edified from unintelligible tongues. Without interpretation, corporate edification is not possible. When tongues are uttered, the tongue speaker is ultimately responsible for the interpretation if no one else provides the interpretation (1 Cor 14:13, 27–28). Church leaders must facilitate space for corporate edification to occur through tongues and the interpretation of tongues.

These nine gifts do not belong to us. They are God's gifts. He apportions and distributes as He pleases. The late evangelist Reinhard Bonnke once said, "The gifts of the Holy Spirit are not badges of honor, but tools for the job."[25] We do not decide which gift we want, but we trust God, the gift-giver. Scripture clearly states that we should ask for spiritual gifts (1 Cor 14:1) and receive them to edify Christ's body. The diversity of gifts apportioned causes us to

22. Trail, *Exegetical Summary*, 133.
23. Ciampa and Rosner, *Corinthians*, 574.
24. Ciampa and Rosner, *Corinthians*, 574.
25. Bonnke, "Gifts of the Holy Spirit."

rely on each other as a body. It cultivates dependency and significance among each member. It destroys the superstar model and encourages healthy dependency on one another. We are scripturally commanded to pursue these gifts so that the body of Christ, and those not yet part of His body, are better served and loved (1 Cor 14:1).

KEY TAKEAWAYS

- Church leaders must remain humble and teachable to properly inform their congregations about spiritual gifts.
- Church leaders understand that spiritual gifts are Trinitarian gifts used in humility and with responsibility.
- Church leaders must cultivate an environment of openness and faith for spiritual gifts to flow in their local church.

REFLECT

1. Why is humility essential when operating in spiritual gifts? How can we cultivate humility and learning rather than arrogance when discussing spiritual gifts?
2. Have you experienced God working in your life through a spiritual gift? What was the impact on you and the other person?
3. Some churches suppress spiritual gifts out of fear. How can we encourage spiritual gifts while balancing order and freedom in the church?

CHAPTER TWELVE

Every Member Matters
How the Holy Spirit Builds a Thriving Body

> *For just as the body is one and has many members, and all the members of the body, though many, are one body, so it is with Christ. For in one Spirit we were all baptized into one body—Jews or Greeks, slaves or free—and all were made to drink of one Spirit. For the body does not consist of one member but of many. If the foot should say, "Because I am not a hand, I do not belong to the body," that would not make it any less a part of the body. And if the ear should say, "Because I am not an eye, I do not belong to the body," that would not make it any less a part of the body. If the whole body were an eye, where would be the sense of hearing? If the whole body were an ear, where would be the sense of smell? But as it is, God arranged the members in the body, each one of them, as he chose.*
>
> — 1 Cor 12:12–18

INTRODUCTION

In the context of spiritual gifts, the apostle Paul utilized the body metaphor to communicate each member's role within the body. Diversity in a member's role does not mean diversity in divine purpose. One goal and purpose is to see God's kingdom expand on the earth. Each person enables that purpose by edifying the body of Christ and empowering the body of Christ to reach those outside the body. Church leaders are called to communicate each member's essential purpose and contribution to Christ's body.

THE HOLY SPIRIT IMMERSES US (V. 13)

The Holy Spirit immerses believers into Christ's body. He is the one who incorporates us and keeps us there. We are not included or excluded because of our ethnic or societal status. Rather, the Holy Spirit creates unity and cohesion from naturally incompatible parts (i.e., "Jews or Greeks, slave or free"). Despite our differences, the Holy Spirit unifies us, testifying to His glorious ability to immerse us into Christ's body.[1] He regenerates us (John 3:5, Titus 3:5), indwells us (Rom 8:11), immerses us (1 Cor 12:13), and seals us for redemption (Eph 1:13–14). He incorporates and establishes us into Christ's body. We are part of Christ's body because of the Holy Spirit's work. As ministry leaders, we must not stand in the way of the Holy Spirit's immersion of people into the body. We must encourage it.

We are not only immersed into Christ's body. God makes us drink of the Holy Spirit. What does it mean that God makes us drink of the Spirit? Upon incorporation into Christ's body, God gives us nourishment or *drink* (ποτίζω), so we are refreshed and empowered.[2] Drinking the Spirit is synonymous with receiving the Holy Spirit's power and grace-gifts. Jesus said it this way in John 4:14: "But whoever *drinks* of the water that I will give him will never be thirsty again. The water that I will give him will become

---

1. Soards, *1 Corinthians*, 264.
2. Gardner, *1 Corinthians*, 542.

in him a spring of water welling up to eternal life." And again in John 7:38–39, "Whoever believes in me, as the Scripture has said, 'Out of his heart will flow rivers of living water.' Now this he said about the Spirit, whom those who believed in him were to receive, for as yet the Spirit had not been given, because Jesus was not yet glorified." Church leaders must create space for people to drink the glorious, refreshing presence of the Holy Spirit. We must not hide the Spirit's life-giving drink. We must not relegate it to small groups. We must not be ashamed of it. We cannot turn the springs of God's presence into the desert of human production.

THE HOLY SPIRIT VALUES EACH MEMBER (VV. 14–17)

Paul highlighted emerging divisions in the Corinthian church based on differing spiritual roles. These various roles should not create competition but cohesion. Local churches benefit from diverse roles. When you are sick, you want to receive healing prayer. When confused about the next steps, you want to receive wise counsel. We need diverse roles that unite to accomplish God's purposes on earth. Diverse roles form the body. That is why Paul said, "If the whole body were an eye, where would be the sense of hearing? If the whole body were an ear, where would be the sense of smell?" (v. 17). Such diversity enables a unified, distinct body with increased reach.

Scripture clearly shows that the church is a body of members, not volunteers. Church leaders must abandon the casual language of volunteers. Dr. Leonard Sweet offers this corrective:

> The church is the work of the Holy Spirit bringing Christ to life, not through "volunteers" but through "members" of the body of Christ. The world has casual helpers called "volunteers" that come and go. The church has committed members and dedicated disciples, active participants in the Lord's mission who are united in their devotion to Christ and each other.[3]

3. Leonard Sweet (@lensweet), "Language matters. That's why if I hear

We are members of Christ's body, serving His mission through the Holy Spirit's gifts. Each member is called to participate in the body by utilizing their grace-gifts. The way we serve may be noticeable or hidden. Regardless, it is valuable. To emphasize this point, the apostle Paul used humor. He compared the foot and ear to the hand and eye. Anatomically, the foot and ear are not esteemed as highly as the hand and eye. Why? They are not as visible. That does not diminish their importance or incorporation in the body. Good luck convincing me that my foot and ear are not part of my body. Each member is invaluable.

This is why attending a local church is so important. We do not attend to spectate. We do not attend to volunteer. We attend to participate as members of the body. Church leaders must emphasize the value of each member's participation. When a member is absent, the body is missing a foot, an eye, or a hand. Local churches are not as effective when their members are not present and participating. This is not an attendance ploy. This is not a pressure ploy. It is a biblical and theological reality. Many blame the COVID-19 pandemic for declining church attendance, but the pandemic revealed an underlying cancer within the Western church—the prevailing methodological approach creates spectators above participators. This causes people to ask, "What does it matter if I'm there since I'm not part of the production?" This question should cut ministry leaders to the heart. How are we addressing these underlying questions that diminish each member's value? Church leaders must communicate and embody a higher, purer, and more glorious theology of each member's role.

THE HOLY SPIRIT HAS A PLACEMENT FOR YOU (VV. 18, 24)

The apostle Paul puts the death nail to church consumerism in this passage. Church members should not survey the ecclesial buffet in their region to determine what they want. The text says God

---

that word 'volunteer' one more time," X, May 18, 2024. https://x.com/lensweet/status/1791854659570921963.

sovereignly arranges members in His body as He chooses. This means God has a placement for each person in His church. We must yield to God's plan when deciding what church to root ourselves in. To reject the Holy Spirit's gifts and placement for those gifts is not rejecting a pastor or a church. It is rejecting God.[4] To resist God's placement in the body is an act of rebellion. God sovereignly and strategically positions members within His body.[5] We must learn how to submit to God's placement, whether we are church leaders or members.

One such placement took place in our ministry in 2021. God opened the door for me to publish an article in a Christian magazine about intergenerational revival. A family in Oklahoma had read this publication for years. When they read my article, they said, "Our hearts came alive. We knew we had to come see the church." The Holy Spirit dramatically confirmed our church as their new home when they came. God is still using them and their spiritual gifts greatly in our church.

We are not in local churches by happenstance. God has placed each member how He wants them to be. Just as He sovereignly constructed the human body, He has masterfully constructed His body with its diverse members and gifts.[6] Each member is interdependent. The New Testament firmly rejects lone-ranger, independent Christianity detached from the body. Dr. Blomberg, offers this reminder:

> In societies where individualism is valued above corporate responsibility, the importance of the metaphor of Christ's church as a body looms large. Paul's emphasis on all of us needing every other believer greatly relativizes any hierarchy of status, rank, or privilege that we might otherwise try to establish.[7]

---

4. Barry et al., *Faithlife Study Bible*, 1 Cor 12:18.
5. Trail, *Exegetical Summary*, 145.
6. Ciampa and Rosner, *Corinthians*, 601.
7. Blomberg, *1 Corinthians*, 252.

May we, as church leaders, cherish and honor the Holy Spirit's distribution of gifts and placement of members in the body.

KEY TAKEAWAYS

- Church leaders must understand that it is the Holy Spirit's job to unite and empower the church by immersing believers into Christ's body.
- Church leaders must avoid a volunteer ministry paradigm and emphasize each believer's significant, participative role in Christ's body.
- Church leaders must be reminded of God's sovereign placement of people within local churches and foster commitment to that placement.

REFLECT

1. How can we create environments where people can "drink" freely of the Holy Spirit's presence and power?
2. How can we actively shift from a "volunteer" culture to a "member" culture in local churches?
3. What systems can church leaders implement to ensure each member feels valued and empowered?

CHAPTER THIRTEEN

Leading with Love
The Heart of True Ministry

If I speak in the tongues of men and of angels, but have not love, I am a noisy gong or a clanging cymbal. And if I have prophetic powers, and understand all mysteries and all knowledge, and if I have all faith, so as to remove mountains, but have not love, I am nothing. If I give away all I have, and if I deliver up my body to be burned, but have not love, I gain nothing. Love is patient and kind; love does not envy or boast; it is not arrogant or rude. It does not insist on its own way; it is not irritable or resentful; it does not rejoice at wrongdoing, but rejoices with the truth. Love bears all things, believes all things, hopes all things, endures all things. Love never ends. As for prophecies, they will pass away; as for tongues, they will cease; as for knowledge, it will pass away. For we know in part and we prophesy in part, but when the perfect comes, the partial will pass away. When I was a child, I spoke like a child, I thought like a child, I reasoned like a child. When I became a man, I gave up childish ways. For now we see in a mirror dimly, but then face to face. Now I know in part; then I shall know fully, even as I have been fully known. So now faith, *hope, and love abide, these three; but the greatest of these is love.*

— 1 Cor 13:1-13

INTRODUCTION

After listing nine spiritual gifts and explaining their importance, Paul presented the proper context for spiritual gifts. While 1 Cor 13 is used primarily for weddings, that is not the context. The context is spiritual gifts within the body. The only proper context for spiritual gifts is love.[1] Spiritual gifts and love are not either-or but both-and.[2] Without love, the most powerful spiritual gifts and extravagant sacrifices amount to nothing. Love is not primarily emotive or thoughtful but action-based. Church leaders must facilitate contexts of biblical love so spiritual gifts find their fullest purpose.

THE NECESSITY OF LOVE (VV. 1-3)

This seeming interruption of Paul's discourse on the Holy Spirit's gifts is an interweaving of spiritual gifts and love. Gifts without love are pointless.[3] Paul offered three comparisons about gifts without love:

1. *Tongues*—"If I speak in the tongues of men and of angels, but have not love, I am a noisy gong or a clanging cymbal" (v. 1). The tongues of men are human languages, like what occurred on Pentecost in Acts 2, and the wisdom and eloquence of human language. The tongues of angels describe a range of angelic, mystical utterances beyond human language.[4] Speaking in tongues to demonstrate spirituality without love is just noise. It is an "empty sound coming out of a hollow lifeless

---

1. Barry et al., *Faithlife Study Bible*, 1 Cor 13:1-13.
2. Gardner, *1 Corinthians*, 557.
3. Trail, *Exegetical Summary*, 168.
4. Trail, *Exegetical Summary*, 169.

vessel."[5] More than noise, Paul's use of the gong and cymbal alluded to the pagan worship practices of the god Dionysus. Paul implied that tongues without love is like pagan worship.[6]

2. *Prophecy, Knowledge, and Faith*—"And if I have prophetic powers, and understand all mysteries and all knowledge, and if I have all faith, so as to remove mountains, but have not love, I am nothing" (v. 2). Paul determined that communicating inspired messages from God, understanding information received through divine revelation, and accomplishing supernatural feats through faith without love are worthless.[7]

3. *Generosity and Martyrdom*—"If I give away all I have, and if I deliver up my body to be burned, but have not love, I gain nothing" (v. 3). Without God's love as the foundation, benevolence and generosity are pointless. In the final judgment, we will not receive credit for actions without love.[8] Even martyrdom without the foundation of love is of no value.

Church leaders, love must be the foundation of everything we do. Without love, spiritual gifts are worthless. They do not benefit the body.[9] Gifts without love only serve the individual and not Christ's body.

Genuine love for God, each other, and our neighbor is the true indicator of spiritual growth. It is more significant than our spiritual gifts or willingness to be martyred for our faith.[10] Jesus affirmed this in Matt 7:22–23: "'Lord, Lord, did we not prophesy in your name, and cast out demons in your name, and do many mighty works in your name?' And then will I declare to them, 'I never knew you; depart from me, you workers of lawlessness.'" Furthermore, Jesus' final teachings to His disciples reaffirmed this reality: "A new commandment I give to you, that you love one

5. Gardner, *1 Corinthians*, 562.
6. Barry et al., *Faithlife Study Bible*, 1 Cor 13:1.
7. Trail, *Exegetical Summary*, 172.
8. Gardner, *1 Corinthians*, 566.
9. Blomberg, *1 Corinthians*, 258.
10. Witherington, *Conflict and Community*, 268.

another: just as I have loved you, you also are to love one another. By this all people will know that you are my disciples, if you have love for one another" (John 13:34–35). One of Jesus' final prayers revealed this same truth: "That the love with which you have loved me may be in them, and I in them" (John 17:26). Dr. Gardner stated,

> Love, as Paul describes it here, is not an extra special grace-gift but is what marks *all* who are possessed by the Spirit. Gifts being exercised in a context where this is not present, where self is first and God and neighbor second or third, where status is sought rather than humility seen, make the person simply irrelevant spiritually.[11]

Love must be the foundation for everything we do. The question remains: What is biblical love, and what does it look like?

THE CHARACTER OF LOVE (VV. 4–7)

Love means various things in our present world. Most definitions are far removed from the biblical definition. In four short verses, Paul used fifteen verbs to describe love. While contemporary definitions focus on emotion, biblical love, specifically ἀγάπη, acts.[12] Biblical love is manifested through action.[13] God expressed His love for the world in the sacrificial act of sending His Son (John 3:16, 15:3, 1 John 4:10). Jesus said the entire Old Testament hangs on action-oriented love (Matt 22:40, Deut 6:5, Lev 19:18). Paul said the whole law is fulfilled in one word: "You shall love . . ." (Gal 5:14). Church leaders must have profound revelation and understanding of the action-oriented nature of biblical love. Let us explore the fifteen actions of love.

1. Love is *patient* (μακροθυμέω). The term *patient* means love receives injuries over a long period without complaint. Some translations choose the term *long-suffering* to communicate

---

11. Gardner, *1 Corinthians*, 562.
12. Verbrugge, "1 Corinthians," 372.
13. Ciampa and Rosner, *Corinthians*, 640.

this reality. Love is not retaliatory, even when provoked. When love is tested, it displays patience despite difficulty.[14] Love remains even-tempered in trying times. Church leader, you must ask for patience that mirrors God's patience toward you.

2. Love is *kind* (χρηστεύομαι). While patience is a passive disposition, kindness is active. Love actively seeks good for others.[15] The Greek term χρηστεύομαι has a storied history. In the second century, according to Tertullian, Romans mispronounced *Christians* (Χριστιανός) as *kindness* (χρηστότης). Why? The Romans believed Christians were "made up of kindness."[16] Do your friends, spouse, family members, and church say you are made up of kindness? What if that became the primary descriptor of church leaders? They model Christ's kindness.

3. Love does not *envy* (ζηλόω). It is not filled with jealousy or resentment against others. It is not displeased with others' success. It does not negatively react when others are promoted. Love does not seek advancement at someone else's disadvantage.[17] Love does not unhealthily desire others' giftings, callings, or life circumstances. Church leader, do you eye other ministries with jealously or tend faithfully to the ministry God has called you to?

4. Love does not *boast* (περπερεύομαι). It is not self-centered. It is not focused on others recognizing your value or gifts. It does not desire people's praise. Love does not elevate one's self-importance. Love does not want acknowledgment.[18] New Testament scholar Gordon Fee says, "It is not possible to 'boast' and love at the same time. . . . [Boasting] wants others to think highly of oneself, whether deserving or not;

---

14. L&N, s.v. "25.168 μακροθυμέω" (derivative of the word for "patience"; L&N, s.v. "25.167 μακροθυμία").
15. Trail, *Exegetical Summary*, 175.
16. Spicq, "χρηστεύομαι, χρηστός, χρηστότης," 516.
17. Barry et al., *Faithlife Study Bible*, 1 Cor 13:4.
18. Barry et al., *Faithlife Study Bible*, 1 Cor 13:4.

[love] cares for none of that, but only for the good of the community as a whole."[19] Love does not seek to prove anything. As ministry leaders, we must live under the law of love, not seeking to elevate ourselves but others. Ask the Holy Spirit if there are any areas where you boast of your successes instead of boasting of God.

5. Love is not *arrogant* (φυσιόω). It is not inflated with its own importance. Love is not puffed up with air.[20] It does not consider oneself better than others.[21] As church leaders, do we seek to impress others with our importance?[22] Love does not show off at other's expense. Church leader, you must not have an inflated view of yourself or your ministry.

6. Love is *not rude* (ἀσχημονέω). It does not behave shamefully, indecently, dishonorably, or disgracefully. It does not fail to show honor, respect, or consideration for others.[23] Love is not rude, shameful, or sectarian. Church leader, do you treat others rudely at home or church?

7. Love does not *insist on its own way* (ζητέω). It does not seek its own desires. It does not demand. Love seeks the interest of others.[24] Love is prepared to give up rights for the sake of others (1 Cor 9). Love is less concerned with its rights and more with serving and benefitting others.[25] Love seeks the good of others, even one's enemy (Mark 10:45).[26] Church leader, do you insist on your way, or do you place others before your preferences?

8. Love is not *irritable* (παροξύνω). Love is not annoyed or easily angered. It does not take offense quickly. It is not on edge.

19. Fee, *First Epistle to the Corinthians*, 638.
20. BDAG, s.v. "φυσιόω."
21. Barry et al., *Faithlife Study Bible*, 1 Cor 13:4.
22. Ciampa and Rosner, *Corinthians*, 645.
23. Trail, *Exegetical Summary*, 176.
24. Trail, *Exegetical Summary*, 177.
25. Gardner, *1 Corinthians*, 571.
26. Ciampa and Rosner, *Corinthians*, 646.

Love does not look to lash out. Do the people around you describe you as easily angered or irritated?

9. Love is not *resentful* (λογίζομαι). Some translations say that love keeps no record of wrongs. It does not keep a record of past wrongs that impact the future treatment of others.[27] That is how God deals with us—"In Christ God was reconciling the world to himself, not counting their trespasses against them" (2 Cor 5:19). Love does not focus on mistakes but releases forgiveness, hoping for God's mercy, not His judgment.[28] Jesus modeled this as He was brutally mocked and executed: "Father, forgive them. They do not know what they are doing" (Luke 23:34). Pause and reflect: Are there times you hold resentment toward others? God commands us to release resentment and love more fully and perfectly.

10. Love does not *rejoice* (χαίρω) *at wrongdoing*. Love does not celebrate unrighteousness. It grieves sin.[29] Jesus put it this way: "Blessed are those who mourn, for they shall be comforted" (Matt 5:4). Contextually, this refers to those who mourn because of their sin. To celebrate sin under the guise of love distorts the biblical definition in preference of culture's definition. Love does not applaud sin. Love weeps at it. Church leaders must be clear about sin, bring light to it, and allow God to issue healing and forgiveness.

11. Love *rejoices with* (συγχαίρω) *the truth*. Love finds joy in the gospel and its message. It is thrilled with righteousness and holiness. Love rejoices in truth because Jesus is "truth" (John 14:6). Love accepts when truth corrects. Does the confrontational nature of God's truth make you shy away from it? Or do you rejoice even when truth counters culture's narrative?

12. Love *bears* (στέγω) *all things*. It puts up with all things. Love keeps going in the face of persecution, misunderstanding,

---

27. Trail, *Exegetical Summary*, 177.
28. Trail, *Exegetical Summary*, 178.
29. Trail, *Exegetical Summary*, 178.

and dishonor.³⁰ Love continues when things are not exciting, fun, or pleasant. There is nothing love cannot face because it never gives up despite hardship.³¹ Church leader, how are you bearing the ministry God has entrusted to you? Are you quick to "throw in the towel"?

13. Love *believes* (πιστεύω) *all things*. Love is not naïve; it "never ceases to have faith."³² Drs. Ciampa and Rosner explain that love "trusts the one who calls us to love others and living out that love for others as a reflection of our trust in him."³³ Therefore, in doubtful cases, love errs on the side of believing rather than suspecting. Love believes in the potential of good, despite the bad, and God's ability to bring good out of evil.³⁴ Even "what was meant for evil, God meant for good" (Gen 50:20). Church leaders must actively side with believing, intentionally rooting out unbelief.

14. Love *hopes* (ἐλπίζω) *all things*. It has no limits to hope. It maintains, keeps, and expects something beneficial. It refuses failure as defeat and places confidence in God's ultimate plan and purpose, no matter how bad it looks. Love remains hopeful because our lives are entrusted to God. That is why 1 Pet 1:3 declares, "He has caused us to be born again to a *living hope* through the resurrection of Jesus Christ from the dead." That is why Paul said in Titus 2:11–13, "Waiting for our *blessed hope*, the appearing of the glory of our great God and Savior Jesus Christ." Love hopes because God's promises are *yes* in Christ Jesus (2 Cor 1:20). Love hopes because our hope is in God, not a situation's outcome. That is why Paul said in Rom 5:3–5, "But we rejoice in our sufferings, knowing that suffering produces endurance, and endurance produces character, and character produces *hope*, and *hope does not*

---

30. Gardner, *1 Corinthians*, 573.
31. Trail, *Exegetical Summary*, 179.
32. Fee, *First Epistle to the Corinthians*, 640.
33. Ciampa and Rosner, *Corinthians*, 650.
34. Trail, *Exegetical Summary*, 180.

put us to shame, because God's love has been poured into our hearts through the Holy Spirit who has been given to us." We cannot hope if we do not have love. The question remains: Is your hope in God, or is your hope in a specific outcome?

15. Love *endures* (ὑπομένω) *all things.* There is no limit to love's endurance. It continues in suffering and persecution. It never stops bearing, believing, and hoping. Jesus exemplified this on the cross when He endured the mocking, abuse, sense of failure, betrayal, and pain. Love endures all things.[35] No matter what we face, we can make it if we have God's love. The more you model your life after Jesus, the more you can endure. Life is difficult. Ministry is difficult. However, our calling demands endurance. If you feel like you cannot endure, lean into Jesus' love and let it infuse you with endurance.

THE PERMANENCE OF LOVE (VV. 8–13)

Paul contrasted the temporal nature of the Corinthians' favorite grace-gifts (prophecies, tongues, and knowledge) with love's eternal nature. It is unending. It never becomes invalid. In the age to come, we will not need grace-gifts. We will not need prophetic oracles or information about the future because we will see God face to face. We will not need tongues because we will have a perfect understanding in God's presence. We will not need knowledge because we will know mysteries we cannot fully grasp on earth. Jesus, the bridegroom, will be united with His bride, the church. He will dwell in our midst (Rev 21:3–4).

Some have misinterpreted verses 9–10 to describe the ceasing of spiritual gifts at the end of the first century. The text, in context, describes the end of the age, not the turn of the century. Dr. Blomberg adds,

> As we have already seen, this violates every sensible reading of verse 12, and it has to distort the actual record

---

35. Ciampa and Rosner, *Corinthians*, 651.

of events throughout church history. Neither tongues nor prophecy nor miracles ceased at the end of the first-century.[36]

When the perfect, completed *goal* (τέλειος) of human history happens at Christ's second coming, the grace-gifts as we know them will cease.[37]

To help us understand the difference between this age and the age to come, Paul used a metaphor: "When I was a child, I spoke like a child, I thought like a child, I reasoned like a child. When I became a man, I gave up childish ways" (1 Cor 13:11). In this age, we speak, think, and reason like children. No matter how much understanding we gain as leaders, we must remember that our reasoning in this age is childlike compared to how it will be in the age to come. We must never become prideful in the estimation of our spiritual understanding.

Paul further described this with another metaphor: "For now we see in a mirror dimly, but then face to face. Now I know in part; then I shall know fully, even as I have been fully known" (v. 12). Corinth was known for making high-quality mirrors; however, even their best mirrors gave imperfect representations of reality.[38] What does this mean? Even with the blessing of grace-gifts, we are limited in this age by our mind and body. We do not yet have our perfected body like we will in the age to come. Therefore, Paul concluded, "so now faith, hope, and love abide, these three; but the greatest of these is love" (v. 13). The fact that love is greater than faith and hope is extraordinary, especially since we cannot please God or come to Him without faith, and faith is hope's aim (Heb 11:6, Rom 15:13). Why is love greater? Faith and hope are not needed in the age to come (2 Cor 5:7, Rom 8:24). Without the revelation of God's love, faith and hope cease to exist.[39] For this reason, church leaders must root their lives and ministries in God's love.

36. Blomberg, *1 Corinthians*, 262–63.
37. Trail, *Exegetical Summary*, 184.
38. Trail, *Exegetical Summary*, 186.
39. Ciampa and Rosner, *Corinthians*, 666.

A helpful evaluative method is a spiritual formation practice based on the revelation that God is love (1 John 4:7–8). Since God is love, we can substitute the word *love* in 1 Corinthians with *God*: "God is patient and kind; God does not envy or boast; God is not arrogant or rude. God does not insist on His own way; God is not irritable or resentful; God does not rejoice at wrongdoing, but rejoices with the truth. God bears all things, believes all things, hopes all things, endures all things. God never ends" (see 1 Cor 13:4–8). To evaluate your spiritual life for development, you can substitute your name for *love*. For example, "_____ is patient and kind; _____ does not envy or boast." Where are you struggling? Where are you succeeding? Where do you need to grow?

KEY TAKEAWAYS

- Church leaders must allow their ministry to be driven by love, not a platform to showcase how gifted they are or how much they can gain.
- Biblical love is not cultural compromise. It is action-oriented in its responsibilities toward God and others.
- Church leaders must remain humble, understanding that even the pillars of faith and hope will pass away, but the eternality of love will remain in the coming age. We must invest in the eternal nature of love.

REFLECT

1. What good actions are you taking that lack the foundation of love?
2. Which of the fifteen action-oriented descriptions of love do you find most challenging to embody?
3. How does the eternal nature of love inform your view of spiritual gifts and their connection to love?

CHAPTER FOURTEEN

Order in the Spirit
Building Up, Not Tearing Down

> *What then, brothers? When you come together, each one has a hymn, a lesson, a revelation, a tongue, or an interpretation. Let all things be done for building up. If any speak in a tongue, let there be only two or at most three, and each in turn, and let someone interpret. But if there is no one to interpret, let each of them keep silent in church and speak to himself and to God. Let two or three prophets speak, and let the others weigh what is said. If a revelation is made to another sitting there, let the first be silent. For you can all prophesy one by one, so that all may learn and all be encouraged, and the spirits of prophets are subject to prophets. For God is not a God of confusion but of peace.*
>
> — 1 Cor 14:26-33

INTRODUCTION

Paul invested three chapters, 1 Cor 12, 13, and 14, describing spiritual gifts. Love is the atmosphere spiritual gifts demand. However, the false depiction of pursuing love and neglecting spiritual gifts dismisses Paul's coequal imperatives to "pursue love, and earnestly desire the spiritual gifts" (1 Cor 14:1). The pursuit of love and the earnest desire of spiritual gifts are both present, active, and indicative verbs. We cannot say one is applicable for today and one is not. Grammatically, they are synonymous. We are commanded to do both. Since that is the case, this chapter will explore how church leaders should facilitate the corporate use of spiritual gifts with biblical order.

SPIRITUAL GIFTS ARE FOR BUILDING UP (V. 26)

The phrase "When you come together" (v. 26) denounces modern attempts to make corporate gatherings optional. Paul did not say if you come together, but when. Cultural Christianity has lowered the scriptural bar with misapplied statements like, "The church is a people, not a building." They are correct to an extent. However, etymologically, the term ἐκκλησία is a compound word from the preposition ἐκ, which means "out from," and the verb καλέω, which means "to be called out from." This term describes being called out from and assembled together. The church is a people called out from the world and assembled together. The church is a people gathered in a place. Therefore, Paul concluded that when we come together, each has "a hymn, a lesson, a revelation, a tongue, or an interpretation" (v. 26). *Each one* does not mean *everyone* in the assembly, but each whose gift is functioning in that particular gathering.[1]

No matter the spiritual gift, whether hymns, lessons (teaching), revelations (prophetic / word of knowledge), tongues, or the interpretation of tongues, they all occur for *building up* (οἰκοδομή). Οἰκοδομή is used throughout chapters 12–14 to describe the act of bringing something closer to completion. When we experience spiritual gifts, they aim to build up weak areas in our spiritual life. They are not meant for people to be awed by our spirituality.

---

1. Trail, *Exegetical Summary*, 235.

They are intended to build others up spiritually. In a particularly discouraging time in ministry, I received a prophetic word that built me up. God used that word to strengthen the areas in my spiritual life that needed help. In public gatherings, church leaders must teach the upbuilding nature of spiritual gifts more than their predictive nature. This creates healthy environments of edification rather than emphases on prediction.

A GUIDE FOR TONGUES AND INTERPRETATION (VV. 27–28)

Paul clearly stated that there should not be more than three messages in tongues during a church gathering. Upon using the gift of tongues, the speaker should immediately ask the Holy Spirit for the interpretation (1 Cor 14:13). If the speaker has previously functioned in the gift of interpretation, they can proceed with greater confidence. If not, Paul urges them to be more cautious in congregational settings. We must remember that Paul deals with the gift of tongues and interpretation in the context of a congregation familiar with each other's spiritual gifts. When you are connected to a church body, you know the spiritual gifts within the body. This allows you to trust that other gifts will function in tandem with your gift(s).[2]

Once a message in tongues is given, another one should not happen until the first message is interpreted. The public use of the gift of tongues is not intelligible without interpretation. It creates a sense of disorder and chaos, creating confusion and uncertainty.[3] If no congregation member has ever functioned in the gift of interpretation, Paul urged the Corinthians not to proceed with the public gift of tongues. Instead, the individual is encouraged to speak to themselves and God. This instruction debunks the idea that the Holy Spirit overpowers the speaker, and they enter

---

2. Blomberg, *1 Corinthians*, 284.
3. Soards, *1 Corinthians*, 298.

an uncontrolled trance. Instead, as the believer yields to the Holy Spirit, the Holy Spirit gives the words (Acts 2:4).

Depending on the size of the church building and congregation, church leaders must tailor systems for the orderly use of the gift of tongues and interpretation. Rather than saying a congregation is too big for them, church leadership can create an orderly process by which someone can utilize these gifts in the public gathering. We do not have a problem finding places for announcements, worship, preaching, and prayer. Why not create an intentional space and process for tongues and interpretation? While it is a high-risk gift, the benefits of edification far outweigh the risks.

A GUIDE FOR PROPHECY (VV. 29–33)

Like tongues, Paul said two or three are permitted to prophesy within a service. After a prophecy is given, the congregation and leaders must weigh what is said. It is important to note that Old Testament prophecy differs from the gift of prophecy in the New Testament. Old Testament prophecy is Scripture. It is wholly authoritative. The gift of prophecy in the New Testament is not authoritative Scripture. It is subjugated beneath Scripture's authority. That is why Paul said in 1 Cor 13:9, "We prophesy in part." When a prophecy is given, it must be weighed and evaluated. We are not judging and evaluating the person but the prophecy.[4] *Weigh* (διακρίνω) means to evaluate by recognizing or perceiving differences. If there are any variances between what is spoken and what is revealed in Scripture, the congregation should reject the prophetic word given. It is not from God. It is in error. Church leaders must be people of the Word and Spirit. We have the responsibility to test words and not unquestioningly accept them. We must not reject them because we dislike them or the message feels uncomfortable. We should reject them when they do not align with Scripture. This requires courageous church leadership that allows space for the gift of prophecy, knowing if it is not correct, they are

---

4. Soards, *1 Corinthians*, 298.

responsible for bringing correction in love. Dr. Blomberg offers six ways church leaders can weigh the validity of a prophetic word:

> 1. Does it glorify God rather than the speaker, church, or denomination? 2. Does it accord with Scripture? 3. Does it build up the church? 4. Is it spoken in love? 5. Does the speaker submit him or herself to the judgment and consensus of others in spiritual humility? 6. Is the speaker in control of him or herself?[5]

After discussing the importance of weighing prophetic words, Paul spoke about the practical need for deference and timeliness in prophetic ministry. Simply put, prophetic words should not be about one person taking an inordinate amount of the service time. If a prophetic word becomes more about someone getting mic time and visibility, it indicates spiritual malpractice. Prophetic words are for edifying the whole body gathered, not for glorifying an individual's spiritual gift.

Like the gift of tongues, Paul said, "The spirits of prophets are subject to prophets" (1 Cor 14:32). This means the prophet is in control of their speech. They can begin and end speaking whenever that is required. While there is an urgency and prompting to speak, the speaker is in control. The gift's function is subjected to and subordinate to the individual.[6] The way we worship and express His gifts reveals His character and nature. The functionality of spiritual gifts reflects what kind of God we serve. He is a God of order and peace, not disorder and chaos. Whether tongues, interpretation of tongues, or prophecy, church leaders are responsible for facilitating biblical order in a way that reflects the God who gives these gifts to edify His church.

---

5. Blomberg, *1 Corinthians*, 285.
6. Witherington, *Conflict and Community*, 287.

KEY TAKEAWAYS

- Church leaders are responsible for ensuring that spiritual gifts are used for congregational edification, not individual showcasing.
- Church leaders must create systems of evaluation and correction for prophecies given in error.
- Church leaders are responsible for structuring and guiding the congregational use of spiritual gifts to reflect God's character and nature.

REFLECT

1. How have you seen spiritual gifts strengthen and edify the church?
2. How do you foster humility in those who operate in spiritual gifts?
3. Are there areas within your church service that are disorderly? How can you address them biblically?

CHAPTER FIFTEEN

Guarding the Message
Faithfulness to the Gospel in Ministry

Now I would remind you, brothers, of the gospel I preached to you, which you received, in which you stand, and by which you are being saved, if you hold fast to the word I preached to you—unless you believed in vain. For I delivered to you as of first importance what I also received: that Christ died for our sins in accordance with the Scriptures, that he was buried, that he was raised on the third day in accordance with the Scriptures, and that he appeared to Cephas, then to the twelve. Then he appeared to more than five hundred brothers at one time, most of whom are still alive, though some have fallen asleep. Then he appeared to James, then to all the apostles. Last of all, as to one untimely born, he appeared also to me. For I am the least of the apostles, unworthy to be called an apostle, because I persecuted the church of God. But by the grace of God I am what I am, and his grace toward me was not in vain.

— 1 Cor 15:1–10

STRENGTHENING THE CHURCH AND ITS LEADERS

INTRODUCTION

After addressing personal and congregational problems in the Corinthian church, Paul dealt with their problematic beliefs about Jesus' death, burial, and resurrection. He reminded them to return to the basics—the true, pure, undefiled Word of God and the unashamed proclamation of the true gospel. Paul put it this way to the Roman church, "For I am not ashamed of the gospel, for it is the power of God for salvation to everyone who believes, to the Jew first and also to the Greek" (Rom 1:16). Church leaders must return to the gospel's power and primacy. We must reject attempts to make the gospel more palatable or attractive and trust the Holy Spirit's work as the gospel is preached.

WHAT IS THE GOSPEL? (VV. 1-2)

Paul apostolically labored in Corinth for eighteen months, founding the church upon the true, pure gospel.[1] After Paul left to plant other churches, Paul's opponents taught "that outside the [law] there was no salvation. To obtain righteousness in the eyes of God, they were requiring that gentile Christians be circumcised and fulfill additional requirements of the Jewish law."[2] What was Paul's response to this heretical teaching of working our way into salvation? "If anyone is preaching to you a gospel contrary to the one you received, let him be accursed" (Gal 1:9). The term *gospel* (εὐαγγέλιον), is loaded with cultural and religious concepts. We must know and remain tethered to it to preach the gospel effectively. In the ancient world *gospel* (εὐαγγέλιον) was often used in a military context. It was the announcement made by the watchmen who would send runners to bring news about the battle's outcome. The runner would carry the news. If it were a positive outcome, they would scream εὐαγγέλιον! The battle has been won. The enemy has been vanquished. The territory has been conquered.[3] In

---

1. Verbrugge, "1 Corinthians," 391.
2. Barry et al., *Faithlife Study Bible*, 1 Cor 15.
3. Friedrich, "Εὐαγγέλιον," 722.

the same way, Paul announced εὐαγγέλιον in Corinth. The battle against the flesh, sin, and spiritual darkness has been vanquished. The battle has been won by the blood of Jesus' cross (Col 2:13–15).

God installed this plan from the beginning and first revealed it to humanity in Gen 3:15: "I will put enmity between you and the woman, and between your offspring and her offspring; he shall bruise your head, and you shall bruise his heel." On the cross, Christ was bruised, beaten, and bloodied. He was "slain, and by His blood He ransomed people for God from every tribe and language and people and nation, and He made them a kingdom and priests to our God" (Rev 5:9–10). "For our sake he made him to be sin who knew no sin, so that in him we might become the righteousness of God" (2 Cor 5:21). As we proclaim this glorious gospel, what should our response and our hearer's response be?

We *receive* it. Paul said to the Ephesian church the gospel is God's gift (Eph 2:8–9). Paul told the young pastoral leader, Timothy, that the gospel is trustworthy and deserves to be fully accepted (1 Tim 1:15). Jesus taught His disciples that the gospel is a seed sown into our lives (Mark 4:20). We hear the message of the gospel and receive it as authoritative and true. We give our lives to this great gift.

Once we receive it, we *stand* in the gospel. What does that mean? We continually believe and entrust our lives to it. We root and ground ourselves in the gospel. We grow in the gospel. The gospel does not end when we pray to receive the gospel. It begins the new life that is "hidden with Christ in God" (Col 3:3). Jesus said it this way: "Everyone then who hears these words of mine and does them will be like a wise man who built his house on the rock. And the rain fell, and the floods came, and the winds blew and beat on that house, but it did not fall, because it had been founded on the rock" (Matt 7:24–25). We stand on the rock of His gospel.

As we receive and stand on the gospel, we are *being saved* by it. Salvation is not just a past-tense experience. It is past, present, and future. When you receive the gospel, you are saved. God is saving us as His grace is actively applied to us in the present moment.[4] God's saving work is also in the future. We will be saved in

---

4. Gardner, *1 Corinthians*, 649.

the age to come when God judges the living and the dead. We were saved. We are being saved. We will be saved. Church leaders, it is our job to preach the whole gospel.

We receive, stand, and are being saved by the gospel if we *hold fast* to it. This means we cling to the gospel. We hold onto it dearly as we allow the gospel to permeate our lives. If we do not do this, Paul said our faith is in vain. How can we know that what we believe is true?

THE GOSPEL IS THE FULFILLMENT OF SCRIPTURE (VV. 3-4)

Jesus' death, burial, and resurrection were carefully and sovereignly planned. People often object to Jesus' death, burial, and resurrection because they were not present to validate it. They feel there may not be enough evidence. They need to touch, feel, and see, as the apostle Thomas did. How can we know this happened? How can we receive, stand, be saved, and hold fast to it? The apostle Peter, who witnessed the empty tomb and the resurrected Jesus, said that Scripture is surer than his experience on the Mount of Transfiguration (2 Pet 1:16-21). He physically heard God the Father. He saw Moses and Elijah. Yet, he said the Scriptures are surer than that experience. How can we be certain? The testimony of the Bible, which was not "produced by the will of man, but men spoke from God as they were carried along by the Holy Spirit" (2 Pet 1:21). Jesus taught this truth in the parable of Lazarus and Dives (Luke 16:19-31). Jesus said, "If they do not listen to Moses and the Prophets, they will not be convinced even if someone rises from the dead" (Luke 16:31). We can trust Jesus' death, burial, and resurrection because of the Scriptures. Here are a few Scriptures that prophetically detail Jesus' death, burial, and resurrection.

Jesus' Death

- Jesus' betrayal to the religious leaders and Romans was prophesied in Zech 11:13 over five hundred years before His death: "Then the Lord said to me, 'Throw it to the potter'—the lordly price at which I was priced by them. So I took the thirty pieces of silver and threw them into the house of the Lord, to the potter."

- The manner of Jesus' death was prophesied in Zech 12:10 over five hundred years before Jesus' death: "And I will pour out on the house of David and the inhabitants of Jerusalem a spirit of grace and pleas for mercy, so that, when they look on me, on him whom they have pierced, they shall mourn for him, as one mourns for an only child, and weep bitterly over him, as one weeps over a firstborn."

- Jesus' language as He died on the cross was prophesied a thousand years before Jesus' death: "My God, my God, why have you forsaken me? Why are you so far from saving me, from the words of my groaning?" (Ps 22:1).

- Jesus' treatment by the Roman guards was prophesied a thousand years before His crucifixion, in Ps 22:18: "They divide my garments among them, and for my clothing they cast lots."

- Jesus' death and suffering were detailed in Isa 53, some seven hundred years before:

    > Who has believed what he has heard from us? And to whom has the arm of the LORD been revealed? For he grew up before him like a young plant, and like a root out of dry ground; he had no form or majesty that we should look at him, and no beauty that we should desire him. He was despised and rejected by men, a man of sorrows and acquainted with grief; and as one from whom men hide their faces he was despised, and we esteemed him not. Surely he has borne our griefs and carried our sorrows; yet we esteemed him stricken, smitten by God, and afflicted. But he was pierced for our transgressions; he

> was crushed for our iniquities; upon him was the chastisement that brought us peace, and with his wounds we are healed. All we like sheep have gone astray; we have turned—every one—to his own way; and the Lord has laid on him the iniquity of us all. He was oppressed, and he was afflicted, yet he opened not his mouth; like a lamb that is led to the slaughter, and like a sheep that before its shearers is silent, so he opened not his mouth. By oppression and judgment he was taken away; and as for his generation, who considered that he was cut off out of the land of the living, stricken for the transgression of my people.... Out of the anguish of his soul he shall see and be satisfied; by his knowledge shall the righteous one, my servant, make many to be accounted righteous, and he shall bear their iniquities. Therefore I will divide him a portion with the many, and he shall divide the spoil with the strong, because he poured out his soul to death and was numbered with the transgressors; yet he bore the sin of many, and makes intercession for the transgressors. (Isa 53:1–8, 11–12)

Scripture clearly foretold the manner of Jesus' death hundreds of years prior. We must fully grasp the Scriptural nature of Jesus' death to communicate the gospel accurately and effectively.

Jesus' Burial

- The same is true with His burial. Jesus' burial was described in detail seven hundred years before it occurred: "And they made his grave with the wicked and with a rich man in his death, although he had done no violence, and there was no deceit in his mouth" (Isa 53:9). Joseph of Arimathea, a wealthy follower of Jesus, asked for Jesus' body and Pilate agreed (Matt 27:57–61).
- Jesus made it clear that Jonah in the belly of a fish was a prophetic shadow of Jesus' burial some nine hundred years before it occurred: "For just as Jonah was three days and three nights

in the belly of the great fish, so will the Son of Man be three days and three nights in the heart of the earth" (Matt 12:40).

Even Jesus' burial was prophesied with certainty. Church leaders must understand the prophetic significance of Jesus' death and burial.

Jesus' Resurrection

- Just as the Scripture foretold Jesus' death and burial, they foretold His resurrection. One thousand years before Jesus' death, Ps 16:10 prophetically declared, "For you will not abandon my soul to Sheol, or let your holy one see corruption."
- Seven hundred years before Jesus' death, Hos 6:2 prophetically records, "After two days he will revive us; on the third day he will raise us up, that we may live before him." At the beginning of Jesus' ministry in John 2:9, Jesus said, "Destroy this temple, and in three days I will raise it up."

Jesus' death, burial, and resurrection are sure because they happened according to the Scripture. That is why we can receive, stand on, be saved by, and hold fast to the gospel. Church leaders can be comforted by this truth. They do not have to devise a million reasons for people to receive the gospel. Western church culture has made church leaders feel they need to jazz up the gospel to attract people. That is not what Scripture asks of us. Church leaders are responsible for faithfully preaching the gospel according to the Scriptures (2 Tim 4:2). For those still seeking additional proof, the apostle Paul offered one more reason people should receive the gospel.

THE GOSPEL IS THOROUGHLY VERIFIED (VV. 5-10)

The gospel's veracity does not simply hinge on the claim of an empty tomb. After God raised Jesus from the dead, Jesus made post-resurrection appearances. Paul provided six specific post-resurrection appearances to validate the claim of an empty tomb.

1. *Jesus appeared to Peter.* The term used for *appeared* (ὁράω) does not describe a vision or spiritually ecstatic experience.[5] Jesus appeared in a physically verifiable way. This caused Peter to jump out of his boat and swim to Jesus. Then Peter ate a meal with Jesus prepared by Jesus (John 21).

2. *Jesus appeared to the twelve apostles.* They hid in a room when Jesus appeared and said, "'Peace be with you.' . . . He breathed on them and said to them, 'Receive the Holy Spirit'" (John 20:21–22).

3. *Jesus appeared to more than five hundred brothers.* This probably refers to the time Jesus went ahead of the women and His disciples into Galilee and revealed himself to five hundred others before they left town and went home after the Passover festival (Matt 28:7–10).[6] Jewish law only required two or three witnesses to verify a claim (Deut 17:6, 19:15). Paul provided more than five hundred witnesses to substantiate this claim.

4. *Jesus appeared to His brother, James.* This is significant because, before this event, James did not believe in Jesus. This appearance inspired belief in James, his half brother, that Jesus was the Son of God and the world's Savior. That is why James entered the upper room with his mother, Mary, after the resurrection. He believed.[7]

5. *Jesus appeared to all the apostles again at the time of His ascension.* They watched Jesus give his last command before ascending into the clouds of heaven. Angels appeared and said, "Why do you stand here looking into the sky? This same Jesus, who has been taken from you into heaven, will come back in the same way you have seen him go into heaven" (Acts 1:11).

6. *Paul shared his own experience with the resurrected Jesus.* As Paul headed to Damascus to torment, arrest, and persecute Jesus' followers, Jesus appeared to him in a blinding light. He

---

5. L&N, s.v. "24.1 ὁράω; εἶδος, ους."
6. Trail, *Exegetical Summary*, 266.
7. Verbrugge, "1 Corinthians," 392–93.

asked him, "Saul, Saul, why do you persecute me?" (Acts 9:4). This experience radically transformed Paul. He renounced his persecution of Christ and became a follower of Jesus.

Scripture thoroughly verifies Jesus' resurrection. Jesus died in accordance with the Scriptures. He was buried in accordance with the Scriptures. He was raised in accordance with the Scriptures. When we preach the gospel, Jesus is revealed to humanity. Just as Paul shared the witness of others' experience with Jesus, church leaders should share how Jesus has encountered them. This witness partners with Scripture's witness to the personal, present power of the gospel. May we never forget to share our experience with God's glorious gospel. May we constantly be reminded of its innate power as we proclaim it.

KEY TAKEAWAYS

- Church leaders must remain faithful to the pure gospel rather than attempting to make it more culturally palatable.
- The gospel is God's power to change lives.
- Church leaders must equip the church to remain rooted in the gospel rather than trying to graduate from it.

REFLECT

1. How can we ensure our preaching and teaching remain gospel centered?
2. How can we help our congregations move beyond receiving the gospel to standing in it?
3. How does the fulfillment of Scripture in Jesus' death, burial, and resurrection strengthen our faith?

CHAPTER SIXTEEN

Opportunities Versus Open Doors
How to Discern the Right Path in Ministry

> *I will visit you after passing through Macedonia, for I intend to pass through Macedonia, and perhaps I will stay with you or even spend the winter, so that you may help me on my journey, wherever I go. For I do not want to see you now just in passing. I hope to spend some time with you, if the Lord permits. But I will stay in Ephesus until Pentecost, for a wide door for effective work has opened to me, and there are many adversaries.*
>
> — 1 COR 16:5-9

INTRODUCTION

Paul concluded the Corinthian letter with his standard shift to personal remarks.[1] In these remarks, Paul often included his intended travel plans. Those plans were subject to circumstantial change or God's redirection.[2] Paul offered great wisdom about the tim-

---

1. Blomberg, *1 Corinthians*, 331.
2. Verbrugge, "1 Corinthians," 408.

ing of God's work. This message is particularly relevant for church leaders discerning open doors and the timing of change.

IT TAKES TIME (VV. 5–7)

Traveling by boat or over mountains was nearly impossible during winter; therefore, Paul intended to travel to Corinth when he could stay for more than a pass-through visit. Paul's pastoral concerns were evident throughout the letter. His initial eighteen-month investment in Corinth of teaching, discipling, and planting the congregation saw a quick degradation. The Corinthians were prideful, discriminatory toward the poor, sexually immoral, petty, heretical, and harmful communal examples. Unfortunately, this is not an exhaustive list.

Paul's sixteen-chapter letter did not resolve all the issues. According to 2 Corinthians, Paul made a painful, brief visit to bring resolution (2 Cor 2:1). He returned to Ephesus afterward and wrote a letter "out of much affliction and anguish of heart and with many tears" (2 Cor 2:4). We do not have that letter. He then sent Titus to resolve these issues before returning for a third visit (2 Cor 8:16–18). This process took time. The Corinthians were under the apostle Paul's apostleship for five to seven years before real change occurred. Paul knew that time was key to their transformation. Paul did not appear in Corinth and have a perfectly functioning megachurch in six months. He had horrific congregational issues within eighteen months that got worse before they got better.

Many denominations, church planting groups, and networks demand immediate change and turnaround from church leaders. Church leadership conferences promise that if you implement their systems, you will see specific outcomes within six to twelve months. This disregards the distinct nature of each church and the time that culture shift takes. There is a reason the letter to the Corinthians differs from the letter to the Romans. The Roman church had different needs than the Corinthian church. Great church leaders understand the need for individualized influence.[3] To see lasting transformation, church leaders must understand how to address each local church's needs uniquely.

Each situation requires two things: (1) individualized consideration and (2) time. Although Paul wrote twenty-nine chapters to Corinth in 1 and 2 Corinthians, in addition to other letters we do not have, he knew they still needed a personal visit. They required time with Paul for a more substantial impartation. Church leader, you may not see the change you desire with immediacy or expediency. But, do "not grow weary of doing good, for in due season we will reap, if we do not give up" (Gal 6:9), and "he who began a good work in you will bring it to completion at the day of Jesus Christ" (Phil 1:6). Just because something takes time does not mean God has abandoned you. It took Corinth nearly seven years to get where it needed to be. If your church is not thriving, if your hope feels lost, be encouraged. It takes time.

THE LORD'S PLAN (V. 7)

Paul's ministry philosophy is depicted in these phrases: *I intend. Perhaps. I hope. If the Lord permits.* His language reflects his submission to God's will. His work and travel were conditional to God's guidance. This is even stronger language than what is found in Jas 4:15: "Instead you ought to say, 'If the Lord *wills*, we will live and do this or that.'" Paul said, "If the Lord *permits* [ἐπιτρέπω]" (v. 7). This term means to give permission from a superior to an inferior.[4] Paul was under God's authority, plan, and direction. Although Paul had plans and preferences, he yielded those to God's instruction.

Church leaders, be careful! We should not presume our plans are God's plans. The prophet Isaiah said, "For my thoughts are not your thoughts, neither are your ways my ways, declares the LORD. For as the heavens are higher than the earth, so are my ways higher

---

3. Kouzes and Posner, *Leadership Challenge*, 29–31.
4. BDAG, s.v. "ἐπιτρέπω."

than your ways and my thoughts than your thoughts" (Isa 55:8–9). The prophet Jeremiah said, "For who among them has stood in the council of the LORD to see and to hear his word?" (Jer 23:18). It is not enough to have good ideas. It is not enough to be strategic. Our plans, ideas, and dreams must be subjected to the Holy Spirit's guidance. Paul knew this well. He was forbidden to preach in Acts 16:6–7: "And they went through the region of Phrygia and Galatia, having been forbidden by the Holy Spirit to speak the word in Asia. And when they had come up to Mysia, they attempted to go into Bithynia, but the Spirit of Jesus did not allow them." Preaching is a noble task. What church leader would assume preaching is a bad idea? A good opportunity does not mean God is opening the door. Too often, we relegate the Holy Spirit's role to steer us away from bad ideas. It is easy to assume our ideas are generally good and that we only need the Holy Spirit's help to eliminate bad ideas. We must move beyond this oversimplification. Even a great idea can be wrong if the Holy Spirit does not permit it. We need His leadership and guidance. Think of Jesus' ministry. God publicly announced Him as His Son with a booming voice from heaven. Then, the Holy Spirit descended upon Him and rested like a dove. I cannot think of a better time to get Jesus' public ministry going. He had all the momentum and public affirmation. Yet, the Holy Spirit drove Jesus into the wilderness, where He was tested. It was not the public affirmation that proved Jesus was ready. It was the wilderness that proved His readiness.

Think of the apostle Peter. Jesus told the disciples God's plan for Him. Peter responded with a rebuke "saying, 'Far be it from you, Lord! This shall never happen to you.' But he turned and said to Peter, 'Get behind me, Satan! You are a hindrance to me. For you are not setting your mind on the things of God, but on the things of man'" (Matt 16:22–23). As we walk with the Lord, we can think our plan is correct. Yet, we can be more aligned with Satan than God. We must set our minds on the things of God and seek His guidance through prayer and Scripture.

Think of the apostle Paul. Jesus Christ Himself appeared to him in a blinding light. Paul had a life-changing encounter. He was praying and fasting when God sent a disciple named Ananias. Ananias prayed for him, and he was healed from blindness, baptized in the Spirit, and baptized in water. Paul was ready! What did he do? He went to the desert for three years for further training and time with Jesus (Gal 1:15–18). We would be tempted to think Paul missed the momentum; however, God's timing often differs from ours.

OPEN DOORS AND OPPOSITION (VV. 8–9)

To this point, Paul emphasized that transformation takes time. Although he planned to visit the Corinthians, he yielded his plan to God's plan. Paul assured them of his preference to visit; however, God opened a wide door for effective work in Ephesus. The term *wide* (μέγας) describes something out of the ordinary in magnitude and intensity.[5] This was a unique door for Paul that God opened. It was *wide* (μέγας) and *effective* (ἐνεργής), meaning it would produce its intended outcome.[6] When God opens a wide and effective door, it is greater than what we can produce and will deliver its intended outcome. We will miss the wide and effective door when we look for opportunities.

I have watched people chase opportunities only to be disappointed by the outcome of opportunities. Chasing opportunity is not a biblical concept. In fact, opportunity chasing is something Satan does. The Bible says in Luke 4:13, "And when the devil had ended every temptation, he departed from him until an *opportune* time." The biblical model is that we make the most of what God has placed before us (Eph 5:16). We yield our plans to His plans. We take up our cross and follow Him (Luke 14:27). We die daily. We trust and acknowledge Him in all our ways, "and He will direct [our] paths" (Prov 3:5–6). He finishes the work He began in us (Phil 1:6). We must not base our lives on opportunities. Instead,

---

5. BDAG, s.v. "μέγας, μεγάλη, μέγα."
6. L&N, s.v. "13.124 ἐνεργής."

we must walk through the open doors where God produces the intended result.

It is essential to know an open door does not equate to a noticeable or preferable door. How do I know? Paul said, "There is a wide and effective door opened to me, and there are *many adversaries*" (see 1 Cor 16:9). When God opens a wide and effective door, the enemy rages. He opposes God's plans and purposes. This wide and effective door was accompanied by Ephesian riots (Acts 19). Paul's gospel preaching produced a transformation that devastated the Ephesian idol-making industry. Paul was not sure he was going to make it out alive. Yet, this was the open door God had for him.

Open doors are often paired with opposition. Abram had an open door of promised offspring, but he faced infertility. Jacob had the open door of marriage and faced a deceitful father-in-law who made him work double the years he agreed to. Joseph dreamed of promise and faced violence, imprisonment, and false accusations. Moses was called to free God's people, and he faced a pharaoh whose heart was hardened toward God. David was anointed king of Israel, faced Goliath, and then spent fourteen years hiding in caves from King Saul. Daniel had visions to see God's people return to their promised land and faced the opposition of exile, where he was renamed and enslaved. Open doors do not mean easy sailing. The most effective doors are often the most opposed. Paul told the Corinthians in his second letter,

> Five times I received at the hands of the Jews the forty lashes less one. Three times I was beaten with rods. Once I was stoned. Three times I was shipwrecked; a night and a day I was adrift at sea; on frequent journeys, in danger from rivers, danger from robbers, danger from my own people, danger from Gentiles, danger in the city, danger in the wilderness, danger at sea, danger from false brothers; in toil and hardship, through many a sleepless night, in hunger and thirst, often without food, in cold and exposure. And, apart from other things, there is the daily pressure on me of my anxiety for all the churches. (2 Cor 11:24–28)

What is God's response to all this opposition? "He who sits in the heavens laughs; the Lord holds them in derision. Then he will speak to them in his wrath, and terrify them in his fury" (Ps 2:4–5). The God who called us faithfully completes the work He started (Phil 1:6). He will never leave us. He will never forsake us (Heb 13:5). He is our shield and defender (Ps 91:4). He promises to carry our heavy burdens and exchange them for His light burden (Matt 11:30). He promises to give us peace (John 14:27). He promises to provide us with a hope and a future (Jer 29:11). He promises He will be with us even until the end (Matt 28:20).

KEY TAKEAWAYS

- Church leaders should stay patient, trusting God's work even when things progress slowly.
- Church leaders must rely on divine guidance rather than strategies, trends, and opportunities.
- Opposition does not mean we are headed in the wrong direction. It may be confirmation that God is at work.

REFLECT

1. How do I handle pressure to achieve quick results?
2. Do I intentionally seek God's direction before making ministry decisions, big and small?
3. How can I better discern the difference between good opportunities and God-ordained open doors?

Conclusion

It is easy to be consumed by the bottom-line metrics of nickels and noses in ministry. God's metrics are often different than ours. The apostle Paul's dealing with Corinth's diverse situations presents this higher, more noble way. These select passages from 1 Corinthians teach us that church leaders

1. utilize historical and theological foundations from Scripture to prepare them for their challenges;
2. lead well because their life and ministry are anchored in God's past, present, and future grace;
3. faithfully preach and rely on God's power through the cross's message rather than their abilities and strategies;
4. serve by guiding others toward maturity developed by God's wisdom, the Holy Spirit's revelation, and Christ's cross;
5. embrace and apply God's wisdom to build ministries in a God-honoring, eternal way;
6. foster spiritual growth and facilitate relational discipleship to ensure churches reflect God's power and love;
7. preach the message of holiness and live a life of holiness so that sin does not contaminate the church's commitment to Christ and its witness to the world;

8. help their congregants attain a higher view of the physical body and its sacred, holy calling since our physical bodies are connected to our personal and collective witness to the watching world;
9. guide others to maturity and holiness by exemplifying sacrificial love for others' spiritual well-being;
10. lead with intensity, intentionality, focus, discipline, and faithfulness, and will, therefore, receive their eternal reward;
11. steward spiritual gifts well, as they emphasize humility, unity, biblical soundness, and opportunity for the personal and corporate use of spiritual gifts;
12. help believers grasp their God-given, Holy Spirit–empowered role as participative members of Christ's body;
13. prioritize biblical love as the motivation and character of all ministry endeavors;
14. create healthy environments for the orderly use of spiritual gifts that edify the church and honor God;
15. embrace, embody, and proclaim the true gospel as the fulfillment of our mission as church leaders;
16. trust God's timing, remain faithful when challenges arise, and rely on God's guidance rather than their plans.

These expositional and experiential revelations remind us of Scripture's ability to address the complex issues church leaders face. May we be people of the Word and the Spirit who treasure Scripture's wisdom and embody its teachings for the sake of the church and the watching world.

Bibliography

Arndt, William, et al. *A Greek-English Lexicon of the New Testament and Other Early Christian Literature*. 3rd ed. Chicago: University of Chicago Press, 2000.

Barclay, William. *The Letters to the Corinthians*. Louisville: Westminster John Knox, 1975.

Barry, John D., et al. *Faithlife Study Bible*. Bellingham, WA: Lexham, 2016.

Blackaby, Henry T., and Richard Blackaby. *Spiritual Leadership*. Nashville: Broadman & Holman, 2001.

Blomberg, Craig. *1 Corinthians*. The NIV Application Commentary. Grand Rapids: Zondervan, 1994.

Bonnke, Reinhard. "The Gifts of the Holy Spirit Are Not Badges of Honor, but Tools for the Job." Sermon, Virginia Beach, VA, Apr. 24, 2016.

Carson, D. A. *Becoming Conversant with the Emerging Church: Understanding a Movement and Its Implications*. Grand Rapids: Zondervan, 2005.

———. *The Cross and Christian Ministry: Leadership Lessons from 1 Corinthians*. Grand Rapids: Baker, 2004.

Ciampa, Roy E., and Brian S. Rosner. *The First Letter to the Corinthians*. Grand Rapids: Eerdmans, 2010.

Crisp, Benjamin. "A Tale of Two Worlds: An Analysis of 1 Corinthians 2." In *Biblical Organizational Spirituality: Christian Faith Perspectives in Leadership and Business*, edited by Joshua D. Henson, 177–98. New York: Palgrave Macmillan, 2022.

Ellingworth, Paul, and Howard A. Hatton. *A Handbook on Paul's First Letter to the Corinthians*. New York: United Bible Societies, 1995.

Engels, Donald. *Roman Corinth: An Alternative Model for the Classical City*. Chicago: University of Chicago Press, 1990.

Fee, Gordon D. *The First Epistle to the Corinthians*. The New International Commentary on the New Testament. Grand Rapids: Eerdmans, 1987.

BIBLIOGRAPHY

Friedrich, Gerhard. "Εὐαγγελίζομαι, Εὐαγγέλιον, Προευαγγελίζομαι, Εὐαγγελιστής." In *Theological Dictionary of the New Testament*, edited by Gerhard Kittel et al., 2:707–37. Grand Rapids: Eerdmans, 1964.

Gardner, Paul. *1 Corinthians*. Zondervan Exegetical Commentary on the New Testament. Grand Rapids: Zondervan, 2018.

Garland, David E. *1 Corinthians*. Baker Exegetical Commentary on the New Testament. Grand Rapids: Baker Academic, 2003.

Gordon, J. Chace. *Grace Empowerment: The Enabling, Transforming Power of God*. Self-published, BookBaby, 2007.

Jiang, Hua, and Rita Linjuan Men. "Creating an Engaged Workforce: The Impact of Authentic Leadership, Transparent Organizational Communication, and Work-Life Enrichment." *Communication Research* 44 (2017) 225–43. https://doi.org/10.1177/0093650215613137.

Johnson, Alan F. *1 Corinthians*. The IVP New Testament Commentary 7. Downers Grove, IL: IVP Academic, 2004.

Keown, Mark J. *The Gospels and Acts*. Vol. 1 of *Discovering the New Testament: An Introduction to Its Background, Theology, and Themes*. Bellingham, WA: Lexham, 2018.

Kouzes, James M., and Barry Z. Posner. *The Leadership Challenge: How to Make Extraordinary Things Happen in Organizations*. 6th ed. San Francisco: Jossey-Bass, 2017.

Louw, Johannes P., and Eugene A. Nida, eds. *Greek-English Lexicon of the New Testament: Based on Semantic Domains*. Vol. 1. Electronic ed. of the 2nd ed. New York: United Bible Societies, 1996.

Pathrapankal, Joseph. "From Areopagus to Corinth (Acts 17:22–31; 1 Cor 2:1–5): A Study on the Transition from the Power of Knowledge to the Power of the Spirit." *Mission Studies* 23 (2006) 61–80.

Prior, David. *The Message of 1 Corinthians*. Downers Grove, IL: IVP Academic, 1985.

Soards, Marion L. *1 Corinthians*. Grand Rapids: Baker, 2011.

Spicq, Ceslas. "χρηστεύομαι, χρηστός, χρηστότης." In *Theological Lexicon of the New Testament*, translated and edited by James D. Ernest, 3:511–16. Peabody, MA: Hendrickson, 1994.

Swanson, James A. *Dictionary of Biblical Languages with Semantic Domains: Greek (New Testament)*. Oak Harbor, WA: Logos Research Systems, 1997.

Thielman, Frank. *Theology of the New Testament: A Canonical and Synthetic Approach*. Grand Rapids: Zondervan, 2005.

Thiselton, Anthony C. *The First Epistle to the Corinthians: A Commentary on the Greek Text*. Grand Rapids: Eerdmans, 2007.

Tozer, A. W. *The Root of Righteousness*. Chicago: Wingspread, 2007.

Trail, Ronald L. *An Exegetical Summary of 1 Corinthians 1–9*. 2nd ed. Dallas: SIL International, 2008.

Verbrugge, Verlyn D. "1 Corinthians." In *Romans–Galatians*, 239–414. Vol 11 of *The Expositor's Bible Commentary*, edited by Tremper Longman III and David E. Garland. Rev. ed. Grand Rapids: Zondervan, 2008.

BIBLIOGRAPHY

Witherington, Ben, III. *Conflict and Community in Corinth: A Socio-Rhetorical Commentary on 1 and 2 Corinthians.* Grand Rapids: Eerdmans., 1995.
Wright, N. T. *Paul and the Faithfulness of God.* Minneapolis: Fortress, 2013.

Subject Index

Apollos, 30–33, 40
apostle Paul, 1, 8, 38, 67, 74, 77, 79, 83, 85, 111, 115, 117, 121

Body
    human body, 6, 51, 52, 54–57, 66, 71, 86, 88, 90, 97, 122
    Christ's Body, 25, 34, 45, 47, 52, 54, 55, 57, 62, 75–78, 80–85, 86, 87, 89, 90, 101, 103, 122

church leaders, 5, 6, 74, 101, 103, 122
church leadership, xi, xii, 34, 102, 115
Corinth, 2–7, 33, 34, 41, 59, 74, 97, 106, 107, 115, 116
cross, 9, 15–22, 24, 26–28, 34, 62, 64, 72, 96, 107, 109, 118, 121

disciples, 12, 41, 78, 84, 90, 91, 107, 112, 117
discipleship, 39–41, 65, 121

faith, 6, 9, 11, 40, 43, 53, 68, 78, 81, 90, 95, 97, 98, 108

faithful, xi, 12, 13, 17–20, 22, 32, 35, 36, 41, 42, 57, 72, 92, 111, 113, 120–22
freedom, 26, 52, 53, 57, 60, 63–65, 67, 68, 71

grace, 8–14, 27, 30, 33, 38, 46, 47, 50, 52, 68, 105, 107, 109, 121
grace-gifts, 74, 75, 83, 85, 96, 97
God's kingdom, 41, 42, 48, 83
God's Word, xii, 31, 40, 71
gospel, 1, 4–6, 10, 12, 17, 20, 21, 25, 37, 38, 66–70, 94, 105–11, 113, 119, 122

healing, 26, 49, 73, 78, 84, 94
holiness, 2, 6, 13, 122
holy, 12, 13, 45–48, 50, 52, 55, 57, 62
Holy Spirit, 26–29, 41, 49, 51, 56, 60, 76, 79–87, 89, 93, 96, 101, 102, 108, 117, 121, 122
hope, 49, 89, 95–98, 116, 120

Jesus, 1, 3, 4, 8–10, 12, 13, 17–20, 24, 25, 30, 32–35, 37, 38, 40, 42, 45, 56–58, 62, 64, 70, 71, 73, 76–79, 83, 84, 90, 91, 94–96, 106–13, 116–18

SUBJECT INDEX

knowledge, 8, 10, 11, 19, 20, 25, 26, 28, 39, 42, 58–65, 73–75, 77, 78, 88, 90, 96, 100, 110

leadership, 7, 13, 15, 29, 117
love, 5, 6, 9, 23, 26, 27, 35, 38–42, 45, 48, 49, 58–65, 68, 81, 88–100, 103, 121, 122

ministry, xii, 7, 17, 19, 22, 36, 43, 49, 66, 67, 72, 77–79, 86, 88, 92, 95, 96, 98, 101, 105, 114, 121, 122
mystery, 23–26, 28, 31, 55, 74

peace, 5–7, 13, 47, 53, 62, 99, 103, 110, 112, 120
Peter, 40, 56, 67, 108, 112, 117
prayer, 60, 79, 84, 102, 117
preaching, 10, 15, 17–22, 24, 31, 32, 34, 66, 69, 71, 72, 102, 106, 111, 113, 117, 119
prophecy, 11, 73, 79, 90, 97, 102, 103
prophetic, 10, 25, 33, 39, 79, 88, 90, 96, 100, 101, 103, 111

resurrection, 6, 46, 95, 106, 111–13

revelation, 10, 17, 19, 20, 24–29, 31, 35, 61, 75, 77, 90, 91, 97–100, 121

sacrifice, 46, 53, 55, 60, 61, 64, 65, 68
salvation, 9, 17, 19, 20, 26, 35, 49, 64, 67–69, 106, 107
Scripture, xii, 7, 27, 38, 67, 77, 79, 80, 84, 102, 103, 108, 110, 111, 113, 117, 121
servant, 31, 32, 67, 70, 76
spiritual gifts, 5, 11, 73–77, 80, 81, 83, 86, 89, 90, 96, 98–101, 103, 104, 122
speech, 8, 10, 11, 20, 41, 42, 74, 75, 103

teaching, 29, 38, 40, 45, 75, 76, 106, 113, 115
temple, 33, 49, 51, 56–59, 111
tongues, 10, 11, 73, 75, 80, 88–90, 96, 97, 100–103

wisdom, 5, 6, 11, 15–24, 26–28, 31, 33–36, 38, 71, 73, 77, 89, 114, 121, 122
worship, 3–5, 40, 53, 59, 61, 63, 64, 90, 102, 103

Scripture Index

OLD TESTAMENT

Genesis
2:24	54
3:15	107
50:20	95

Exodus
3	56
13	56
14	56
16	12
40	56

Leviticus
19:18	91
21:6	62

Deuteronomy
6:4	62
6:5	91
17:6	112
17:17	48
21:23	18

1 Samuel
4:21	34

2 Samuel
6:1–11	18

Psalms
2:4–5	120
16:10	111
22:1	109
22:18	109
90:1	34
91:4	120
119:11	xii
139:17–18	27

Proverbs
3:5–6	118
8:1, 20–21, 22–24	77
12:1	38
19:2	39

Isaiah
9:7	13
29:14	18

SCRIPTURE INDEX

Isaiah (continued)

40:13	27
53	109–10
55:8–9	116–17
66:2	xii

Jeremiah

23:18	117
29:11	120

Hosea

6:2	11

Zechariah

11:13	109
12:10	109

NEW TESTAMENT

Matthew

3:8	11
4:20	107
6:11	12
6:27	12
7:14	48
7:22–23	90
7:24–25	107
10:8	42, 78
11:6	38
11:30	120
16:18	13
16:22–23	117
17:20	78
18:20	13
22:40	91
25:23	70
27:57–61	110
28:7–10	112
28:18–20	40, 120

Mark

3:14–15	40
4:1–20	17
4:20	107
4:26–27	32
10:45	32, 68, 93

Luke

4:13	118
8:9–15	68
9:26	21
14:27	118
16:10	19
16:19–31	108
19	35
23:24	94

John

2:9	111
3:5	83
3:7	47
3:16	91
4:14	83
4:18	78
7:38–39	84
8:7	77
13:34–35	91
14:6	94
14:26	27
14:27	120
15:3	91
15:13	64
17:16	47
17:26	91
20:21–22	112
21	112

Acts

1:11	112
2	89
2:4	102
2:24	19

SCRIPTURE INDEX

2:37	21
4:30	79
9:4	112–13
9:5	64
9:15–16	1
13:8–10	79
15:29	59
15:36–18:22	1
16:2	68
16:6–7	117
16:6–10	1
17:16	61
17:19–34	19
17:22–34	20
17:28	62
18:1–18	5
18:3	2
19	119

Romans

1:16	17, 21, 106
6:1–4	9
6:13	54
8:11	83
8:19	25
8:24	97
8:29	25
11:33	36, 28
12:1–2	55, 57
12:3	9
12:3–8	77
12:18	20–21, 48
15:13	97
16:25–26	25

2 Corinthians

1:20	95
2:1	115
2:4	115
2:5–11	49
3:2–3	9
4:3	68
4:4	70
5:7	97
5:19	94
5:21	107
8:16–18	115
10:4	75
10:10	41
11:24–28	119

Galatians

1:8	17
1:8–9	67
1:9	106
1:15–18	118
2:11–21	67
2:20	25
5:14	91
6:9	116

Ephesians

1:13–14	83
1:22–23	13
1:23	34
2:8–10	68
2:8–9	107
2:19–22	33
3:4–6	25
3:17	56
4:11	77
4:11–16	33
5:16	118
5:23	34
5:27	48
5:31–32	55

Philippians

1:6	116, 118, 120
2:5–8	32
2:9	19
3:4–6	2, 68
3:4–11	9
3:20	47

SCRIPTURE INDEX

Colossians
1:15–20	62
1:16	62
1:18	13
1:25–26	25
1:27	56
2:13–15	107
2:15	19, 26
3:3	107

1 Thessalonians
1:4–5	68
1:9	61

1 Timothy
1:13–14	9
1:15	107

2 Timothy
1:6	11
2:2	41
3:7	19
3:16	38
4:2	19

Titus
2:11	9
2:11–13	12, 95
2:12	12
3:3–8	9
3:5	83

Hebrews
11:6	97
12:6	41
12:11	39
12:12–17	47–48
13:5	120

James
1:5	77
4:15	116

1 Peter
1:3	95
1:18–19	56
2:9	9
5:4	70

2 Peter
1:16–21	108

1 John
2:27	27
4:7–8	98
4:10	91

Revelation
2:20	45
5:9–10	107
13:8	25
20:11–15	13
21:3–4	96
22:13	34

www.ingramcontent.com/pod-product-compliance
Lightning Source LLC
Chambersburg PA
CBHW072150160426
43197CB00012B/2330